FRIDAY AFTERNOON

Reflections on the Seven Last Words

Neville Ward

Published for The Upper Room
by Winston Press

BY THE SAME AUTHOR
*The Personal Faith of Jesus as Revealed
in the Lord's Prayer*

Cover design: Art Direction Inc.

Cover photo: Cyril A. Reilly

Copyright © 1984, 1976 by J. Neville Ward.
Originally published in Great Britain by Epworth Press. This edition
is published by Winston Press, Inc., by arrangement with Epworth
Press.

"Questions for Group Discussion and Personal Reflection" by
Marie Livingston Roy, copyright © 1984, The Upper Room,
Nashville, Tennessee.

Library of Congress Catalog Card Number: 83-60875

ISBN: 0-86683-744-2 (previously ISBN: 0-7162-0259-X)

Printed in the United States of America

5 4 3 2 1

Order # UR 487
The Upper Room
1908 Grand Avenue, P.O. Box 189
Nashville, Tennessee 37202

Published for The Upper Room by:
Winston Press
430 Oak Grove
Minneapolis, Minnesota 55403

To
Kenneth Brian Wilson

ACKNOWLEDGMENTS

The author and publisher are indebted to the following for permission to reprint copyrighted material:

Darton, Longman and Todd Limited, London, for an excerpt from *The Foolishness of God* by John Austin Baker, published and copyright 1970 by Darton, Longman and Todd Limited.

Doubleday & Company, Inc., for an excerpt from *A Rumor of Angels: Modern Society and the Rediscovery of the Supernatural* by Peter Berger, copyright © 1969 by Peter L. Berger.

Grove Press, Inc., for an excerpt from *A Personal Anthology* by Jorge Luis Borges, translated by Irving Feldman, copyright © 1967 by Grove Press, Inc.

Harcourt Brace Jovanovich, Inc., for excerpts from *Four Quartets* by T. S. Eliot, copyright 1943 by T. S. Eliot, renewed 1971 by Esme Valerie Eliot.

Macmillan Publishing Company, for the poem "The Two Parents" from *Collected Poems*, Rev. Edn., by Hugh MacDiarmid, © Christopher Murray Grieve 1948, 1962.

Penguin Books Ltd., London, for excerpts from *The Cloud of Unknowing,* translated by Clifton Wolters (Penguin Classics 1961), copyright © Clifton Wolters, 1961; and an excerpt from *Peer Gynt* by Henrik Ibsen, translated by Peter Watts, copyright © Peter Watts, 1966 (Penguin Classics, Revised edition 1970).

G. P. Putnam's Sons for an excerpt from *Waiting for God* by Simone Weil, copyright 1951, renewed 1979 by G. P. Putnam's Sons.

CONTENTS

PREFACE

WE DISLIKE LIFE for disappointing and hurting us. Yet every day some part of life goes wrong—harmlessly, absurdly, sometimes frighteningly. A sane prescription for happiness would be to expect trouble (trouble of one kind or another being the general rule) but also to be certain that it is possible to reach fulfillment through it.

Jesus explained his own idea of happiness to a world no happier or less happy than ours, only to meet with malice and violence. This hostility was in part due to the fact that he gave too positive a role to suffering. The way he talked made you think that when life asks us for more than we can give, or takes from us more than we can do without, it is out of that giving, that letting-go, that happiness is principally made.

Since then his more earnest and expert followers have been persistently drawn to this part of his mind. They have the same report on experience for everyone who asks for it; it is that whether one makes a success or failure of life depends almost entirely on one's attitude to its hurt and disappointments. It is not that there is any merit in these pains. It is difficult to see them as life's friends; but they defeat us and turn us from God so often that the work of happiness must necessarily lie principally with them.

How Jesus himself met suffering, as confirming or denying what he said about it, has naturally attracted the eyes of the world. Particularly in his dying on the cross the Christian imagination has seen the message and the man as a marvelously consistent whole.

It is recorded that Jesus spoke seven times that Friday afternoon while he was dying. They are seven moments in which the huge ideas that he had continually discussed with himself and others were focused into an unforgettable concentration and simplicity. Christian meditation continually returns to them. Whatever we believe or do not believe about God we have to learn to live with hurt and disappointment as we learn to live with cold in winter and heat in summer. Christian spirituality has recently been much concerned with the joy of commitment, certain excitements in the life of prayer, and the ethical implications of compassion. But the spiritual life is as large as life. Each generation has significant preferences in the aspects of Christian life it selects for emphasis. There never seems to be enough consideration given to such sensitive areas as success and failure in the negotiation of life's regular tendency to disturb and dismay, to the inevitable tension in even admirable encounter with its mystery and wrong, to the possibility that even if many people live lives of quiet desperation they may yet be ready to learn courage, maturity, hope, like lessons, if someone will help. The prayer of distress must be the only prayer that many people can recognize as theirs.

For the prayer of distress the seven last words of Jesus mark the route to be traveled to discover for oneself the meaning he gave to suffering and to find the grace to say "Father, into thy hands I commit my spirit." The meaning of the cross, now as ever, needs continual exposition by the theologians. Another way of approaching it, however, could be by suffering, and by praying that in one's sufferings the seven words may in some sense be said again. The following chapters form a brief essay in the spirituality of atonement.

To look deeply into these seven pictures, so that they affect both our understanding and our feelings, becomes the meditative spelling-out of what at another time can be contemplated in simple attention, as when one prays before the blessed sacrament or a crucifix or sings with the Church "When I survey." It is good to survey the cross, but what is implicit in its image must be unfolded in detailed personal meanings and relevances if we are to be seized by it and drawn into its continuing presence. Its continuing presence is God's continual making evil good.

That kind of meditation is of the greatest service to contemplation. When our mind is still before the blessed sacrament, where what we traced successively in meditation is concentrated in the immediacy of a single sign, that wordless attention will be increasingly filled with real presence. Indeed that presence will be the more real in all the places haunted by it, in the Eucharist, in the Passion music of Bach, in any requiem, painting, icon or line of verse whose symbols and metaphors bring to mind the name of Christ and his face of tragedy and hope.

NEVILLE WARD

Westbere
Canterbury, England
1976

1

FORGIVING

And when they came to the place which is called The Skull, there they crucified him, and the criminals, one on the right and one on the left. And Jesus said, "Father, forgive them; for they know not what they do."

St. Luke 23:33-34

WE NEVER KNOW FULLY what we are doing, what exactly is going on in what we are doing. The whole of the past is involved in every human situation. Most of it is infinitely diluted and untraceable. Some recent event is so clearly present that we are tempted to think it explains the bit of life it seems to dominate. However, we do not in fact understand. A hundred echoes from distance, countless relations with the remote and the near, provide the clinging ambiguity that makes life so fascinating and at the same time so difficult to disentangle that it is obviously given only to God to see clearly why anything happens.

To look within means to find a similarly misty landscape. Our successes and failures all have some relation to unconscious strivings and fears. These have roots that go so deeply into our mysterious inwardness that some of the reason why we managed this, succumbed to that, will always escape us.

There is the world of the spirit to be taken into account. We never know whose love, whose prayers, whose fidelity in similar stress to some idea of good, brought up the strength available to us to the amount sufficient for our sustaining some loneliness, some depression that otherwise would have thrown us. All local honorings of the good (say, someone somewhere doing a good day's work) may add to the general power of good. And it may well be that evil forms a similar system, that wrong choices, indulged glooms, relished hates all have a way of belonging, and together form a network of spreading malevolence whose gathering power strengthens and is increased by each of our aggressive doings or withholdings.

We do not know what we are doing in the sense that we cannot know the whole tale of its results. The insignificant stir made by the stone casually thrown into the sea of life merges with the broad tide of things and is lost to us. But we know that life has a tendency to get out of hand. If we could have seen further into the consequences we would often have acted or spoken differently.

Our community's past, our own inexpert assessment of life's encouragements and disappointments from infancy until now, our current needs and goals, the unpredictable ambivalent fellowship of the spirit, all go to make the intriguing density of that atmosphere in which we do what we do at any moment.

As we grow older
The world becomes stranger, the pattern more complicated
Of dead and living. Not the intense moment
Isolated, with no before and after,
But a lifetime burning in every moment
And not the lifetime of one man only
But of old stones that cannot be deciphered.[1]

Since there is much more than we know going on in what is going on, when things go wrong, have gone wrong, however carefully we sift the evidence, we shall never arrive at that place of accusing light where we know who is to blame and who is not to blame. Some part of life's wrongness we may justly think is in no way our responsibility. Wrongs that were done a hundred years ago cannot be laid at our door. However, that is true only retrospectively. Prospectively, from the moment we become aware of it, how we respond to a world that contains that wrongness is very much our responsibility. To exist at all is to be in principle accomplices or redeemers of the past. If we are taken over by our resentments and fears we give hostility and anxiety a new base of operations for wrecking life further. If we try to put some distance between ourselves and the rage or terror we feel, argue the pros and cons of their ambiguous role, and attempt to understand them, we shift the balance of evil in the world and become places where reason is struggling through and a happier tomorrow is being prepared both for ourselves and the world.

Where this happens in human relationships, where someone bears injury without retaliation and without his love becoming even just a little frightened and therefore more cautious and reserved, so that there is now simply a richer love where that evil has been done, we call that miracle forgiveness.

The people in whom it happens, in whom the chain of pain, resentment, retaliation is broken because their love is not damaged but continues undiminished, are people who take away the sins of the world. With Christ, whether they acknowledge him or not, they form the Lamb of God so mysteriously and thankfully celebrated in the Eucharist. They do not explain evil and suffering and guilt, they do something infinitely better. They become places where there is the forgiveness of sins and the evil of life is no longer thrown in God's face.

To train the power to love so that it can sustain wounds and disappointments must be in part to train the imagination's sensitiveness to the cloud of appearances in which we live, and to learn how to assess what is going on under the surface of life, particularly under the surface of our own life. The rejection of religion that is a feature of some students' college life may simply mean that they are involved in putting the necessary distance between themselves and their parents or perhaps more fiercely in retaliating against them for what seemed to them the suffocating pietism of their childhood home. By a similar mechanism, in adult life, again and again dissension in marriage activates the stored wraths of childhood; and mothers are attacked through wives and fathers through husbands. Many wounds are inflicted and received simply because someone's general dissatisfaction with life must express itself and the one who happens to be near enough to be hurt is simply unlucky. Most common of all is the situation in which we do not realize that the person we are attacking stands for some part of ourselves that we deeply wish was not there. Jesus was able to forgive his persecutors. On the whole his followers have not been able to be so gracious, perhaps because the murderers of Jesus stand obscurely for something in ourselves that we condemn.

He said they did not know what they were doing. They certainly did not know who he was, that he was the voice of truth.

If they did recognize truth in some of what he said it was apparently too fresh and disturbing for them to absorb. The situation is a common one. Jesus himself said that there is truth whose moment has come and there is truth that cannot be borne just now. We are often particularly hostile to truth that is just beginning to impress us and, in our reluctance to admit the need to change an attitude, we want to land a last blow out of perverse loyalty to the ideal we know we are going to surrender.

Training the ability to love will involve a careful look at our use of the mind's capacity to make judgements, especially adverse judgements. It is possible to make an unbiased adverse judgement about another person, but it needs great skill. It is extremely difficult to make a strictly unbiased criticism of someone unless you do in fact love that human being and wish him nothing but good. Two factors account for the difficulty; they are distressingly frequent; one is the secret intent to hurt, the other the desire for superiority. However certain we are that we are making an objective and sympathetic criticism, it is almost inevitable that some form of aggression, some intent to wound will be mixed up with our judgement if the person we are criticizing has wronged us at some time in the past, even though it is the distant past, or failed to give us what we wanted in the way of interest, appreciation or affection. And if there are features of the other person's life and circumstances which life has not got round to giving us—success, abilities, intelligent taste—the odds are that, in spite of our conscious desire to be just, there will be a twist of sharpness in what we say.

And in that inner world where we live with thoughts we cannot escape, if we have demands on life that have not been met and feel that the world owes us a few items, if at times we play around rather long with despair, there is bound to be lurking in the hinterland of our personalities the desire to hit out at life. However successful we are at controlling that desire we shall not prevent its giving just that corrupting touch of hostility to all our critical judgements by which they cease to be expressions of disinterested opinion and become vehicles of our stored-up bitterness, weapons to serve us in our secret, sullen struggle with a world we are against.

The act of criticism gives us temporarily a superior position and feeds our confidence; and so it easily becomes a means of elevating oneself at others' expense. One of the motives that make gossip so appallingly irresistible is the desire for that increase of prestige which comes from being in possession of a morsel of news that no one else knows and imparting it generously to an interested and attentive audience. The desire to say clever and surprising things about people springs from the same need to impress. Even if we have no need to raise ourselves in the opinion of others we may yet wish to feel rather more assured in our own opinion. To sum up things and people and make discerning judgements about them always leaves a slight feeling of power and silence for the moment the sense of inferiority. All is not well with anyone who must go in for frequent depreciation of things and people, even though with wit that is often decidedly amusing. And in such incidents our malaise shows, because what we say reveals clearly how it is with us. Every day through the conversation of mankind there are a million fulfillments of that saying of Jesus about what is thought to be secret being brought to light.

Theoretically the Church is the forgiven and forgiving community; and Christians should be good at forgiving, thinking so much about it as they do. However, that is the kind of theory that does not easily transplant from the pages of library books to the pains of beating hearts. Some people are in fact good at forgiving, whether committed to it like Christians or not. Buoyant and extroverted temperaments seem to find it easier than reflective and withdrawn types who often cannot stop their memories fingering old wounds.

Sometimes to keep wounds hurting by withholding forgiveness is not a matter of deliberate choice but a kind of compulsion, yet springing from the source of healing within us. We perhaps are unwilling to admit that some minor humiliation hurt us deeply because we suspect it may be yet another humiliation to realize that we can be so hurt by such small-scale events. So we tell ourselves that there is nothing to forgive. But, at a deeper level within, the holy spirit of life knows we are playing with self-deception and keeps bringing the mind back to the scene of pain, and the pain itself, to persuade us that nevertheless there is work to be done there if we are to be free of it.

On the other hand, we can withhold forgiveness and keep an injury alive simply as a kind of drug. There is a limit to the number of defeats one can take (that's to say, what one thinks are defeats). As this limit approaches, people usually do not realize how hopeless they have begun to feel. They now find an odd satisfaction in feeling victimized by life. They begin to need to suffer, to accumulate the evidence with which they can charge life in their continual arraignment of the universe for treating them so ill. There is a degree of unhappiness beyond which more of the same thing actually in some sense relieves, because the edges of the self's identity then become blurred in a general sense of wretchedness and we feel the slings and arrows less. Whenever the inability to forgive seems to be unreasonably intense or prolonged it is often because the offense was not an isolated incident to be dealt with on its own merits but was the means of activating a hopelessness we did not suspect was our morose secret. Our hostilities are complex and deceptive. Underneath their sharpness and destructiveness there is often a softer thing, a sadness about life that could in fact be the easier level on which to begin asking questions. Certainly hope seems to be the only route by which faith can pass into love.

In the New Testament there is a question about the hopefulness of love. The case is brought to Jesus of a man who has done wrong and been forgiven six times, and has offended again. Is that just about the limit or ought he to be forgiven a seventh time? Jesus' "seventy times seven" is his way of saying that love does not keep the score.

The point is apparently illustrated in St. Matthew's gospel[2] by the story of the unmerciful servant. It is a revolting story that does not illustrate the point at all. Jesus was pleading the wisdom of endlessly repeated forgiveness. The story is a story of violence. A man owing a fantastically huge debt is forgiven. He then throws a man into jail who owes him quite a small sum. He is reported to his benefactor who is so furious that he condemns him to torture until his original debt has been paid in full, which must mean, in view of the fantastic sum involved, that he virtually condemns him to endless torture.

What the story illustrates is the world of violence, and that there is no end to that world. It is true that, for someone who has been forgiven much, to refuse to forgive a small matter is outrageous behavior. The question is what is the sensible thing to do about it. Outrageous behavior can be met with punishment or it can be met with forgiveness. Punishment successfully maintains the vicious circle of injury and retaliation. It is not certain but it is at least possible that forgiveness might break that vicious circle. It would not break it, though, unless it was repeated again and again, until the offender became convinced that he himself was loved, in himself and for himself, and could accordingly relax his tensions and begin to question his defensive cruelty. Jesus was a man who sensed more than anyone the endless waves of pain that roll across the human world and had no confidence that wrath is any use in this situation, and he tells Peter that he had better settle for the idea of endlessly repeated forgiveness. A limited forgiveness is ultimately shown up as still part of the world of violence. Sooner or later it turns to violence. Unlimited forgiveness, so Jesus believed, is what God himself is; and so people of faith can trust it to straighten out the world into a place of love and freedom.

It is a mistake to interpret the idea of a love that does not calculate as meaning a love that does not think. For example there are situations in which it is necessary to assess responsibility, because the needs of someone who is entirely a victim of life, of some inherited defect or some distortion of personality through intolerable events, are different from those of someone who is able to learn from experience and can register the appeal of more efficient living and respond to it. But love is most characteristically itself when making such assessments.

Nor does it reveal its true self in the decision "to forgive and forget." That could be just another form of calculating. It is often unrealistic. It is easier to forget kindnesses than injuries. And wounding experience should not be summarily dismissed. It needs to be absorbed, worked deep into our life by our honestly acknowledging our pain and our fury, and perhaps (if we are in receipt of such insight) our share of responsibility, and then relating it to whatever wisdom and compassion we have learned. If we omit this homework we cannot forget the matter, in spite of our good intentions. We simply stack it away somewhere in the mind where we cannot see it. There it waits, to add its own supply of resentment to all our future annoyances and wraths.

The thought that "to understand all is to forgive all," when allowed to dissolve slowly in the mind, has some effect on resentment. If we knew all the antecedent experience, the humiliation and deprivation, the resulting insecurity, and the temperamental constitution of the person whose behavior has caused us alarm or grief, we would be able to explain many of his actions. But to understand does not necessarily enable you to bear. The "all" that you now understand may be as unpalatable as ever. And you still have on hand the work of dealing with your unfulfilled wishes concerning this person and the way life should go for you.

In any case, one of the situations in which love is most clearly seen is when it continues undiminished through injury or alarm it does not come anywhere near understanding. Many Christians have found that loving God must have that strand in it if it is to hold; for some, indeed, the love they can give him is mostly just that bewildered, obstinate thing.

An uncalculating love is not the same as unconditional love. Unconditional love is admirable in the beautiful inequality of a mother's love for her baby but it has no place in the adult world except in the neurotic dream. To want to be loved regardless of what one does is to want to go home to the infantile. Love cannot bear literally all things without itself becoming much reduced. If someone behaves intolerably and is unwilling to alter, or wishes to be loved without having to make the effort of loving in return, such a person cannot be loved in the fullness of the word's meaning. Kind people may put up with it for a while until they drop away, or just wait in hope and the prayer of hope. But that does not look like love to the person who wants unconditional love.

Even God's love is not unconditional. It is not helpful to say, as many an evangelist has claimed in overselling the gospel, that God loves us whatever we do. God's love is like the wind of the spirit of life. It blows one way and one way only, towards fuller and deeper life for ourselves and the world. If we go in some other direction we find it in varying degrees against us. We experience the intransigence of things, as though they meant to slow us down and defeat us. It may be theologically sound but it is also academic to say that nevertheless God still loves us. We certainly cannot know that, know him as love. The Bible is so sure of this that it argues that we can only know him then as wrath.

In human love we cannot know other people's love unless we can love in return. We can know some less mutual aspects of love, for example their patience and loyalty, but most of what love marvelously gives is received only in the communion of mutual giving.

So forgiving is not love unaffected by what people do, which could only be an insensitive and mechanical affair. Forgiving is love managing to continue though injured or dismayed or mystified. It continues not by forgetting the injury and dismay or dismissing the mystery to some other world where we shall understand everything but by including it in its appreciation of the one who is loved. This new aspect of him, revealed by what he has done, is understood as part of his reality, indicating perhaps new features of his need, his fear, his mistaken attempt to defend some area of his being from exposure. Where such revelation, though painful, does not produce hostility or even make love more cautious or apprehensive but adds to its depth and equips it for more sympathetic loving—it is forgiveness that is happening there.

The more pain there is, the stronger the proof of love. This must be the reason why Christians persist in seeing the revolting cross as the image of love. Pain is an integral part of convincing love because, in order to convince, love must be tested and be seen to hold. An idyllic, unsuffering love would tell the world practically nothing about love, even though its lovers were as radiantly happy as children in sunlight.

Becoming able to include and absorb injury, without the usual deposit of resentment and fear of being hurt again, is a talent not acquired in the direct encounter with injury. The major work to be done is in a wider field.

We would not so quickly turn on life or be afraid of it if we saw it as the presence of God, as the presence of love, as therefore a likable thing on the whole, to be trusted to come out right, to be so arranged that, given the willingness to work at it, we can discover what to do to help it to come right. It seems that prayer is for acquiring this pleasant attitude to experience.

This attitude has to be acquired because most of the time we live by a more anxious scheme. Long before we thought of praying, or thought about the claims of different attitudes to life, two tendencies had become installed in our minds—to be angry when our peace and joy are interrupted, to be afraid of future attack on what we consider necessary to our peace and joy. The roots of these two tendencies reach down into our infancy, so that every adult experience of loss and threat is linked to (and may even be mysteriously fed by) tears and terrors long forgotten.

There are continual and sometimes ridiculous signals that these two tendencies are operating—the sudden drop in morale for no apparent reason, the annoyance at a remark made by someone you have already decided is quite harmless though helplessly garrulous, the gloom evoked by some drift of memory bringing into your mind the picture of some humiliation in your school days. Still, such fervent trivia are signposts on the road to self-understanding.

St. Matthew pictures Jesus as beginning his teaching with unexpected congratulations on the poor. Most people ask the question of life in the form "how much can I get?" Jesus seemed to be asking people "how much can you lose?" Fortunate people, in his view, are those who by some grace are not given to grasping at compensations or have learned to let go, as though if they let go enough they will suddenly find the keys of the kingdom in their hands.

For its training in forgiveness the mind needs to be fed with Jesus' understanding of life as always in God's hands and as meant for learning faith and love. As people learn to love and trust men and women and life itself they develop a double assurance—that so much is wrong that there is an infinity of work for love to do, and that nevertheless it is right that there is so much for love to do. The more they sense the rightness the more they receive grace for the work. They learn to accept and respond to things as they are, a mixture of the beautiful and the outrageous, so that one is continually being called to stop and admire and be grateful and is likely the next minute to have one's heart wrung with one or other of life's ridiculous muddles or terrible injustices.

This acceptance and response are prior to explanation. Jesus lived in a mental world that was not disturbed or invigorated by asking whether God exists or life has a meaning or by discussing the problem of suffering. It did not seem a proper thing for humans to doubt God's existence or question his ways. He certainly never even began to think that the pain of life was an argument against faith. He regarded it as an occasion for work, for doing God's will, so that glory might be revealed in it.

It is not clear that having the talent to read and think some way into the *problem* of suffering is any help at all in the *work* of suffering efficiently and productively. It ought to be some use but the evidence for this is not strong. The rewards of suffering seem to come not to man as a challenged intellect, sorting it out, but to man as trusting and loving and holding on.

It is as possible to live like that today as it was in Jesus' day, as possible and as difficult. It is made possible by faith in God as obscurely present in every situation, whether joyful or painful, offering the generosity and imagination to make it an occasion for love, a kind of illumination and in the end a reason for gratitude.

So we never find Jesus blaming God, but always, though not always easily, discovering grace to trust God to see him through. He seemed to know he must lose but was ready for this, was good at losing, not clinging desperately to any of our precarious hopes. Yet for the end, for the whole amount of things, he had immense hope, hope in God, the first and last voice, but likely to speak in what is quite incidental and marginal, so that you had to be careful not to dismiss anything or anyone.

This deep trust that the whole sum of things is in the hands of a loving Father is set out as the characteristic Christian posture before experience in the prayer Jesus taught his friends. That is not to say that the Lord's Prayer makes everything clear. It is not an explanation but an attitude. The first cry from the cross is a gloss on the two words "Our Father."

When Jesus prayed "Father, forgive them, they do not know what they are doing" he lifted up to God the whole tangled and unfathomable pattern of human ignorance and fear and injury and retaliation in which he was so hideously caught. He stated his faith again that it was all within that fatherly love whose purpose is to make a kingdom of forgiveness and reconciliation.

We have beautiful and important anticipations of that great forgiveness here and now, whenever one human being forgives another or is forgiven by man, woman or God. But there is a

vast area of the unforgiven and the apparently unforgiveable in
this world. There are people who do not yet want forgiveness
and die not wanting it. There are those who are incapable of
forgiving, like a brutalized boy who is so damaged that he
grows into an inadequate or psychopathic adult; he cannot understand what forgiving means, and no one can forgive on his
behalf. There are some situations of fantastic horror, like the
Nazi attempt to exterminate the Jews, that seem to go beyond
anything we can attribute to any known person or persons. And
there may be a dark infinity of distress reaching out from some
of our own smallest wrongdoings. We cannot scour the world
for all those who have been injured or will yet be injured by our
cruelties and failures and make amends to them all. The fact is
that the word of full forgiveness cannot be heard by anyone in
this world. If this world is all there is it cannot be heard at all.

However, it is Christian faith that ultimately, beyond history,
it will be heard by all. In the world of time the immeasurable
wrongness of life must remain incomprehensible. Jesus finally
referred this greatest mystery of God's purpose to transform all
life in the fulfillment of his heavenly kingdom. That kingdom
comes as people come to see God as forgiving love, always
present, always overcoming evil with good. In the relief of
realizing that this is the way things are, that it is possible (only
the certainty being withheld from us) that everything is working
for the deepest good of all, people can unclench their hands
and drop their sense of being owed this and that by life, as
though hearing a great providing voice saying that there is enough
and to spare. As anxiety loosens they become free to give. The
spirit of man in freedom is by a marvelous necessity a giver and
lover. As the Bible ends, in a bewildering dazzle of images and
symbols for that which all its packed religion discerns ahead of
us, there is a recurring image of a final gift which is an unending
love, the gift of praise to him who will at last be seen to have
done all things well.

The prayer of forgiveness is a way of seeing that releases
love. Though it is a desire for others' good and therefore an

intercession, at a deeper level it looks more like contemplation. It is faith seeing those who have wronged us, and ourselves, within the great reconciliation of God's kingdom and trusting our belief that he is at work to bring in that kingdom of truth and affection. To pray this in stillness and trust is to receive from God a further light, that our resentments and fears are to be transformed; they are not essential to our humanity; we are not doomed forever to hurt and destroy one another. In such hope we might begin to question their claim to tyrannize over us and so find their hold on us loosen.

This is certainly one of the ways in which prayers of intercession are answered. No prayer for others can be justified that does not involve the one who prays in allowing himself to be drawn into God's purpose to redeem the broken and wasted years. John Austin Baker has argued persuasively for this way of seeing intercession as a form of contemplation:

> We are not engaged in creating or producing anything, but in becoming aware of what is already the fact, namely that God is immediately and intimately present both to ourselves and to the ones for whom we are praying. Our task is to hold the awareness of this fact in the still centre of our being, to unite our love for them with God's love, in the quiet but total confidence that he will use our love to help bring about the good in them which we both desire. In technical terms, therefore, intercession is a form of that kind of prayer known as "contemplation," with the special feature that here we contemplate not God in himself but God in his relationship of love towards those whom we also love. . . .[3]

To pray in this way for someone who has wronged us, holding that person steadily in the gaze of faith, is exactly the same as praying for someone we love, only much harder. It is clearly one of the forms of prayer that are more like work than prayer as usually understood, and it must, if it is true to itself, lead into further work, such work as the situation requires for the relationship to come right. It is good to be realistic about this.

Nothing is to be gained from assuming that, because prayer is a recognized part of the Christian life, we can do it, or ought to be able to do it. Our injuries are certainly not the most transparent part of our experience. Some of them we unconsciously provoke, so that we mysteriously collaborate with those who wound us. These may be the hardest to forgive. Some of them provoke a perfectly legitimate anger. It is not, then, the anger that is in question but what we propose to do with it: sometimes we shall act with good sense, sometimes with such grace as can only be a sheer gift from God, but sometimes we shall simply retaliate or otherwise make fools of ourselves. The struggle to see as far as we can into all this is worth the effort. And every honest self-assessment is meditation well done. To attempt to deny that one is hurt, or to continue bearing situations that deserve protest because such gentleness and unselfishness are thought to be Christian, is to allow false guilt to suppress the real, living self. The price of this is considerable. So much control is needed that one cannot put oneself wholly into anything but must let out what one thinks and feels in small, personally unrepresentative, submissions to what is respectable.

Some people smother their protests so efficiently that they begin to feel smothered themselves, but at such depth that all that shows is a compulsive need to extricate themselves from they do not know what. So they forever sit in the back row of life or near the door, careful not to be too much involved, at ease only if they can escape quickly.

The prayer of forgiveness is precisely for preventing such impoverishment of one's life. But it involves the recognition that we are not proficients at loving and that where we cannot organize our aggression productively, by faith or with the help of others, we shall just have to be angry.

Some of our unwillingness to forgive is due to our unreadiness to accept this, to see that we have feet of clay like everyone else. It is created and fed by unacknowledged perfectionism. For various reasons (a pietistic upbringing, an inability to take failure, a need to be above criticism) we expect too much of ourselves and consequently too much of other people, too much of life altogether so that it kicks back in one disappointment after another. It would be good if we could make a pact with ourselves not to blame ourselves or others or life for not meeting the obsessional hunger for the absolute that God has planted in us. It would be an agreement to forgive earth for not being heaven. Every relationship, pleasure, ambition, piece of work done, must have its core of discontent, must at some point fail us, because we are made to want something always just beyond it. What it is God alone knows. All we know is that if we had not this infinite want we would settle for the here and now, and, loving it, necessarily hate death, or else disapprove of it all.

2

HOPING

One of the criminals who were hanged railed at him, saying, "Are you not the Christ? Save yourself and us!"

But the other rebuked him, saying, "Do you not fear God, since you are under the same sentence of condemnation? And we indeed justly; for we are receiving the due reward of our deeds; but this man has done nothing wrong."

And he said, "Jesus, remember me when you come in your kingly power."

And he said to him, "Truly, I say to you, today you will be with me in Paradise."

St. Luke 23:39-43

A CHARACTER in one of Saul Bellow's novels speaks of suffering as "a form of gratitude to experience or an opportunity to experience evil and change it into good." But this requires talent. "You have to have the power to employ pain, to repent, to be illuminated; you must have the opportunity and even the time." Some religious people think this opportunity, somehow to make use of his suffering, comes to everyone "if only in the last moments of his life, when the mercy of God will reward him with a vision of the truth, and he will die transfigured."[1]

It is not difficult to see at the back of such thoughts the man whom Christian imagination remembers as the good thief. He is described by St. Luke as a man very much at odds with life, in his last round of trouble, unable to escape, whose suffering unexpectedly brightens with a remarkable light. He is given one of the revealing glimpses of reality that actually come to most people periodically when in a summary moment your mistakes become clear but the truth is clearer—the truth you might have followed. A sort of folklore gives this privilege of illumination to the drowning. This man belongs in that group of people, those *in extremis* who struggle with the drift and summons of ultimate things.

Reports that come from experience of the depths suggest a hidden hopefulness. To come to the end of the line in one sense or another often means discovery about oneself and insight into truth that apparently are available only in this superficially hopeless situation. There is no certainty about this. Sometimes the end is the end as far as we can see. But to many people it has meant at last seeing the way through. This last friend of Jesus is shown as almost at the last minute seeing something new about who is in the right and who is in the wrong in this obscure world. He is able to strike up some kind of understanding with the man with whom he is sharing doom. In the flame that suffering sometimes lights in the mind he sees that there is more to living and dying than he had guessed and that that more has much to do with the man at his side. Somehow, somewhere, the tables would be turned and this defeated man of Nazareth would be seen to be one with the true dignity and strength of life. He rides into death on the back of this new-found hope and trust, "Jesus, remember me when you come in your kingly power."

And Jesus said, "Truly I say to you, today you will be with me in Paradise."

Hoping and trusting in Christ means going on to the next thing with Christ, with God's living word. For this man the next thing is death, but he goes into it with Christ. What is beyond is anyone's guess. The language which man has painfully, excitedly devised for giving meaning to his mundane interests and dreams provides the means for expressing little more than our hopes and fears about that. Actually, it is immaterial whether the word "paradise" means the realm where the righteous dead wait for resurrection or is a word for the final thing, the blessedness of heaven. What matters for faith is that to be with Christ is what believing and hoping in him bring you. Whatever is next for you comes to you with him—which is why it has been said that so to die, "in the Lord," is a blessed thing, but no more blessed than so to live.

It has always been part of Christian cheerfulness that it is possible to ignore God and the Church and the guidance of the Bible, and the stream of life that pours from the sacraments, and the warnings of misused experience, all one's life, and then at the end turn to God and home at the last minute. However, that is not the sort of truth one can live on.

We do not know now that we shall want to turn to God then, or shall be able to turn to him then. Much will happen to us between now and then, to change us in unimaginable ways. If we are lucky enough to want him at the end, when we have nothing to offer him but the burnt out fire of our love, we shall have him. He is the one who always comes when he is wanted. But we certainly do not know whether or not we shall indeed want God then, even think of him then, the self we shall have become by so much doing without him all the way through.

However, to make too much of this is to start playing shivery
games like old-style evangelists. It is less than Christian to
argue the advisability of turning to God now for what one will
secure, or alternatively avoid, then.

If it is good to know God by faith it is simply a good that is
known now, in the present. If we come to God late we must
have missed much good that we could have enjoyed had we
been more fortunate. It cannot be helped when it happens that
way, and there is no doubt that we have him when we come to
him at the end of the day, but it is not all the same whether we
come to him soon or late.

The point is made best in the world of love. People who love,
are truly in love, begrudge the time when they did not know
one another or had not met. Some of the most beautiful poems
and songs are written on this tenuous theme that is as old as
youth. Similarly, if it is good to find a meaning in life and to
see it making sense round the man of Nazareth, it is simply
good, it is good now, and that part of our life in which we were
not interpreting life and living it the Christian way was less
good, less happy, more confused, with many chances of deep
experience necessarily not taken. When St. Augustine finally
gave himself to God he wished it was not so late in the day.
"Too late have I loved thee, O thou beauty of ancient days yet
ever new!" So he wrote in his *Confessions* in the refined distress that has haunted the Christian mind ever since. He was
thirty-two years of age.

There is much more in the man who shares death with Jesus
than a sinner who has a lucky break at the end. One of Jesus'
particularly complicated thoughts about life is found in St.
Matthew 11:12, "The kingdom of heaven suffers violence and
men of violence grab it." He may have been thinking of contemporary revolutionaries, trying to realize their political dream
by violence. He may have been, more generally, thinking of
the energy and enthusiasm and passion required to win anything that is worth while, whether it is a new social order or
God himself. It is not the inert, the casual, the spent, but "men

of violence," of longing and hope and perseverance and daring
who are able to seize the kingdom.

This criminal, with his just-in-time moment of vision, is in
this sense a man of violence, a revolutionary idealist and en-
thusiast, fired by the thought of the world he passionately wanted
to see, a man of hope. Many saints have been made out of "men
of violence" who at last found God. The allegiance they trans-
fer from one set of aims to a more complete and convincing
vision of life represents the resources of an available and giv-
able self. This man is given to us not as a finished creature
running for cover but a man of hope who has found his truth at
last and uses all his hope and fire to identify with it.

> That day
> At his task of dying crucified,
> He heard, amid the crowd's mockery,
> That he who was dying at his side
> Was a god, and said to him blindly,
>
> *Remember me when you inherit*
> *Your kingdom,* and the inconceivable voice
> That shall judge one day each man's merit
> Promised him from the terrible cross
>
> Paradise. Nothing more was said
> Until the end came, but history
> Shall preserve from death the memory
> Of the afternoon on which they died.
>
> Oh friends, the innocence of this friend
> Of Jesus, the candor that moved him
> From the ignominy of his end
> To ask for Heaven and receive it,
>
> Was the very same that so many times
> Had hurled him into sin and bloody crimes.[2]

One of the forms of the holy spirit that must not be quenched
is this inner force in virtue of which people are able to give
themselves to life. To be able to give oneself carries no guarantee of virtue or success. Such giving may be utterly mistaken

or simply glorious, in association with bloody crimes or the
service of Christ, but as elemental readiness of response it is
the essence of man's vitality. Borges thinks of it as innocence
and candor perhaps because like Jesus before him he sees it
particularly vividly in children who have an open-ness to experience not yet spoiled by fear nor reduced by the wisdom that
is just preconception and tired expectation. It is what enables
us to meet experience with unfailing interest, able to attend, to
wait on it, to ask questions of it, to observe, to participate, to
be ready to find in situations all the varied meanings that imagination and willingness can find in them. This is the blue heart
of the flame of hope. The people in whom it burns will never
be mere victims of experience. They may well be temporarily
overwhelmed by suffering but in due course they will regain
the initiative as individuals who are giving their own meaning
to experience instead of puppets who are being manipulated by
life's malevolence.

This hope seems to ebb and flow through the years and just
now is a receding tide in the west. The pressures of a mass
civilization produce a tired generation, content to be enter-
tained and diverted, not expecting to be called upon for any
positive gesture, ready to complain and so still apparently wanting something, though invariably settling for money, unable to
do much about loving.

The contemporary unwillingness to consider religious matters is often due to the fact that people suspect that the conclusions to which life has quietly been leading them are not very
hopeful. Whatever raises the question of a meaning (if any) to
life directs them to this part of their being where for some time
sadness has been accumulating like blood seeping through a
bandage. The resulting confusion is a distress that on the whole
they prefer to avoid.

A generation living rather helplessly in this way, aware of
its feelings but not free to live them consciously and deliberately, is bound to have difficulty with its sufferings. Joy is
something you can, if you wish, just let happen to you, but

suffering is a load of work that must be done. It is work that requires goodwill and seriousness, indeed the deepest interest, none of which are available to us if hope is not.

The sociologist Peter Berger is intrigued by this aspect of human life, that essentially man is a being who indefatigably hopes. "Human hope has always asserted itself most intensely in the face of experiences that seemed to spell utter defeat, most intensely of all in fact of the final defeat of death."[3] Men and women certainly fear death, but by an intriguing mental incapacity they are unable to imagine their own. They suffer the death of people they love but always with protest. They can consider the possible end of terrestrial life with a fine surge of irrational contempt, as did Joseph Conrad in his essay on Henry James: "When the last aqueduct shall have crumbled to pieces, the last airship fallen to the ground, the last blade of grass have died upon a dying earth, man, indomitable by his training in resistance to misery and pain, shall set this undiminished light of his eyes against the feeble glow of the sun."

Berger sees this extraordinary faculty of hope, with its ability to outstare death, as one of the awkward features of human experience that do not fit easily into a purely this-worldly understanding of life but seem to require a wider scheme:

> There seems to be a death-refusing hope at the very core of our *humanitas*. While empirical reason indicates that this hope is an illusion, there is something in us that, however shame-facedly in an age of triumphant rationality, goes on saying "no!" and even says "no!" to the ever so plausible explanations of empirical reason. In a world where man is surrounded by death on all sides, he continues to be a being who says "no!" to death—and through this "no!" is brought to faith in another world, the reality of which would validate his hope as something other than illusion.[4]

The possibility that this power to say "no!" to death is in some way linked with a transcendent world that includes death and is infinitely greater than it, greater in richness of being and

in power of action, is the most important feature of its interesting persistence in human life. The power to say "no!" to death
is the same power that enables man to say "no!" to all the
penultimate endings of various kinds that are intimations of
death and, in a sense, rehearsals of it, an ended love affair,
disgrace, marriage breakdown, incapacitating illness, bereavement, all experiences that seem to say "All is over for you. All
that matters in your life is finished."

To say "no!" in such experiences is not to deny the experience itself nor its catastrophic severity (any more than the
Christian denies the fact of death itself). What is denied is the
voice in all such experience that says to the sufferer "*You* are
finished, you have no future; life is not worth going on with
now."

What makes it possible for people to defy the voice of death
in the evil day is the presence of meaning. It does not matter if
their particular meaning is made of flimsy stuff in the opinion
of others, it can yet do its work of keeping them roped to life.

One of the commonest questions asked of priests and min-
isters by those severely battered by experience who are not yet
packed up and heading for bitterness is "Do you think there is
some purpose in what I've been through? Can it possibly be
any use to God?" If they can see meaning in their troubles,
better still, if they can in some sense offer their pain to God
knowing it will not be despised, immature and not very profound as it is, they are ready to hold that meaning in their sights
and make that unpretentious offering a little longer.

Religious meaning is independent of the apparent goodness
or evil of experience. Indeed it is found exactly among people
who have been through much of the outrageousness of existence rather than those who have not been put to major tests.
Faith is a matter of living through situations in as much love,
joy and peace as we can receive from God because God wishes
life to be so lived and his presence enables it to be so lived. If
the situation is an agony and is so lived it becomes a particularly

vivid occasion of the glory of God. It is in this sense that suffering can be seen as a special offering to God for his use, because suffering is so widely seen as marking the absence of God.

Christians in trouble are persons particularly involved in working through, in proving in their lives, this faith that painful situations, when interpreted as particularly important opportunities of serving God and receiving from God, are more manageable than when understood in other ways, more manageable and more productive of personal good.

This is the essential Christian idea. It is not goodness or unselfishness or even love as so many people seem to think. Many people get around to managing some of that. The essential Christian idea is that pain lived through for God and with God leads to a resurrection, to a new kind of existence altogether in this world and the next.

People who have no orthodox religious faith can still find meaning in their sufferings. Life can make sense for people in a fantastic diversity of ways many of which still work though current experience may be hideous. And when everything seems to have fallen in because of the removal of some relationship or purpose that was loaded with years of memories and difficulties and heavenly satisfaction it is still possible to arrange one's life in a new pattern that restores interest and value to it and makes each day worth its give and take. People have managed their re-adjustment with the single help of the crazy idea of dignity, which by some luck or grace remained clinging to them when some storm swept away everything else that mattered.

However, the question in distress, at its deepest, does not concern life's meaning or its supposed lack of meaning but the presence of hope, the willingness to try life another way.

Christian understanding of life provides many considerations that make the experience of disaster more manageable, but the way in which "we are saved by faith" is not primarily a matter of what faith does for us at the time the blow falls. It concerns the imaginative openness to life and the patient willingness to look for God's hidden presence which faith has involved us in cultivating over the years in one experience after another of loss, of life's tendency to close in and reduce.

If the question is raised as to what Christian hope is hoping for, the answer is that the Christian in distress accepts his desolation as what it is, the rending of the self in humiliation and in loss of a whole world of happiness, but *also* as destined to be absorbed and changed into growth and sustenance of personal life. The destructive event and the broken heart can be considered the wretched bread set before me by life or myself (in my madness or mistake) or even the devil. The central sacrament of life is that transubstantiation by which what the devil puts on the table becomes the Lord's body, and then substance of our mortal body, the hope of glory.

What form life will take when the devil's bread has become the body of Christ is not accessible to the imagination in advance. Perhaps for long enough it will continue to look like the devil's bread, that is to say, the withdrawal of love, the family disgrace, the dreaded diagnosis, the death which at first overwhelmed the sufferer. The New Testament conviction is that deep within it can be known and experienced as a present certainty of life's goodness and innocence and promise, "that we are children of God." What is beyond that is not given us to see yet, but it is hinted that it will be a deepening and intensification of the same good thing.

It is in fact essential to Christian hope that what is hoped for is not clearly defined. Gabriel Marcel, in his book *Homo Viator*, considers a man who is seriously ill, who imagines that everything is lost for him if he does not get well, identifying recovery with salvation. While, however, he is immersed in such imaginings and expectations he has not truly begun to hope. He is merely held in the grey world of desire and fear. There is a point of view from which it is clear that everything is not necessarily lost if there is no cure. To find it is to enter

upon a certain liberation and relaxation that are characteristic
ingredients of hope.

> . . . in so far as I make my hope conditional I myself put up
> limits to the process by which I could triumph over all succes-
> sive disappointments. Still more, I give a part of myself over to
> anguish; indeed I own implicitly that if my expectations are not
> fulfilled in some particular point, I shall have no possibility of
> escaping from the despair into which I must inevitably sink. We
> can, on the other hand, conceive, at least theoretically, of the
> inner disposition of one who, setting no condition or limit and
> abandoning himself in absolute confidence, would thus tran-
> scend all possible disappointment and would experience a se-
> curity of his being, or in his being, which is contrary to the
> radical insecurity of *Having*.[5]

Deepest happiness, surest security are matters of being, not
of having. It is precisely in the world of having that insecurity
hides, along with fear, jealousy, resentment and the long litany
of miseries from which in their moments of seeing human beings
have always wished to be delivered. Anyone clearing a space
in the mind for the idea of being, for the tender care of attitudes
and loves and of what goes out from us rather than what comes
in, is doing the remote preparation for the prayer of hope. And
even if we do not believe in Jesus we shall have that marvelous
influence hidden in our lives, to be noted one day, like a water-
mark visible when you hold it up to the light.

Hope is most clearly seen when it is completely detached
from having, when it is simply an individual's response to life
as that infinite being to whom one is conscious of owing everything, both the bad and the good in his life, on whom one
cannot impose any condition whatever, in whom as continual
change and renewal one lives and moves. When life is lived in
this way it seems that loss and gain themselves become ambiguous, like actors switching roles, and the discoveries and new
beginnings somehow carry the familarity of home. Life's goods
seem preserved or restored in a continuing experience of movement and change quite beyond our power of explanation and

description. One is offered a kind of flexibility before life, a willingness to let things vanish because it just could be the case that there will never be one lost good.

> This aspiration can be approximately expressed in the simple but contradictory words: *as before, but differently and better than before*. Here we undoubtedly come once again upon the theme of liberation, for it is never a simple return to the *status quo*, a simple return to our being, it is that and much more, and even the contrary of that: an undreamed-of promotion, a transfiguration.[6]

When disaster falls and the outraged heart sometimes longs for death, the voice within that cries for the end of it all is in one sense the voice of truth. The self whom the sufferer is must indeed die, because the self cannot absorb this overwhelming trouble. In such situations we can die in one of two ways: by committing suicide, or by letting this dreadful experience do the killing, letting it rub out the self we were and make a new person—the sort of person who has entered a dimension of experience unknown before; for there will now be a new range of sympathy and compassion available the us, some new knowledge of how to give a hand to those who scan their unremunerative sea of difficulty and begin their consent to sink. We may perhaps even acquire some fresh vision of the world of responsibility. That type of grace could never be defined beforehand as the object of hope, but it is in fact again and again the discovery and result of true, open-ended hope. So it can be said that when a man's life falls in ruins what is not destroyed is exactly the liberty to hope in this authentic way— that, accepting and going through, he will not return to what he was before the blow fell but can expect "an undreamed-of promotion, a transfiguration." Another word for this is "resurrection."

The ability to hope is not the result of effort but of contemplation. What is contemplated is summarily indicated in various ways for the Christian mind. There is an abundance of images—Christ in glory, the assumption of the Blessed Virgin Mary, the mysterious grace by which (as St. Paul said) things are drawn together to unite in the production of good, the anonymous voice of the man who discovered "if I make my bed in hell, behold thou art there." The landscape of Christian prayer is strewn with signs of the life that rises out of dying; and to stare long and hard at those emblematic expressions that most fully carry this assurance is the due occupation of the praying mind.

It is not required that the image be examined and understood. It has only to be held until it seems to expand and fill the mind, which then becomes a form of loving rather than a kind of thinking. This practice of holding one thought and allowing the surrounding penumbra of ideas and images with their attendant feelings to fade away simply through lack of attention is a way of praying recognized in all the major religions of the world. It is marvellously expounded by the fourteenth-century English author of *The Cloud of Unknowing*.

In Christian experience there are times of distress when this contemplative stillness is not simply a form of praying but the only possible way of living. Sufferers are advised then simply to hold in faith to this deep theme of death and rebirth and the possibility that this is their inner situation. They may find that they cannot entertain that view of their pains, but if they have dwelt on it, continually refreshed their vision of it, in Eucharist and solitary reflection, it will come as grace to them when effort fails to reach it. There are some lines of the poet T. S. Eliot which are well worth memorizing in which he has beautifully expressed the thought that in this openness and waiting, without what is expected from God ever being named, loss and deprivation are transformed into a joy in which it seems life's earlier experiences of beauty and youth and the timeless are given back to us:

I said to my soul, be still, and wait without hope
For hope would be hope for the wrong thing;
    wait without love

For love would be love of the wrong thing; there is yet faith
But the faith and the love and the hope are all in the waiting.
Wait without thought, for you are not ready for thought:
So the darkness shall be the light, and the stillness the
    dancing.
Whisper of running streams, and winter lightning.
The wild thyme unseen and the wild strawberry,
The laughter in the garden, echoed ecstasy
Not lost, but requiring, pointing to the agony
Of death and birth.[7]

The twentieth century as it runs into its last quarter is showing signs of a serious hope-deficiency. Perhaps it is becoming
ready to consider suggestions as to the leaks through which our
ability to be enthusiastic about the prospect before us has been
trickling away. The thought of death must always be high on
such a list.

Jesus seems to have been able to hold that thought in his
mind without the distress it causes us, mainly because he knew
of a bigger reality than death, one that could be trusted to look
after death. The idea of God as the ruling presence in one's life
was what absorbed his daily thoughts and interest. He recommended it as an antidote to anxiety, and with great seriousness
because anxiety is life's chief depresser, quencher of hope and
thief of joy. The more God rules in our lives the more we shall
trust and love. The more we trust and love the more we shall
hope to go on with trusting and loving forever, even beyond
death. Trusting God is trusting that we are continually in his
care and that our dying is one of the forms of his caring. Our
dying is not some inane fight between God and death for each
one of us that death wins. Trusting God, living in faith and
love, include accepting the fact that we cannot see how it can
be—it certainly looks as if we altogether die—but we believe
that trusting and loving are raised to continue on another shore
and in a greater light. This belief is not arrived at by inference
from events in this world. It is to be traced to the fact that
trusting and loving simply add up to that kind of serene expectation. The thought of death, the most disconcerting, indeed

outrageous, thought that man can think, is not dealt with by an argument, much less by the bizarre trivia which form the pathetic haul from the adventure of psychical research. It is found, however, that trusting and loving reduce its pretensions and threats rather well.

People can lose hope because of being unable to stand any more discouragement from their failures, like incessant innuendoes in a conversation with someone who knows too much about you. Jesus' prescription for that section of the hopeless is repentance, though the word has gathered so much portentousness it does not now seem a word of grace that could ever have proceeded from the mouth of one whose ideas with their passion and fresh air were listened to with pleasure by ordinary people.

There is a time when one's skill at self-delusion no longer impresses even oneself. It is a time of what the religious call grace. The gift it brings is the realization that in some important respects we have got life wrong, that some of our misunderstanding of life, and the fears and hates this misunderstanding has provoked, are our own fault, but we see a better way of negotiating experience and we propose to turn into it now.

We often need to be helped to effect this change of mind. We certainly cannot manage it under threats or under a sense of personal humiliation and self disgust. In an imperfect world, sometimes looking a decidedly tragic one, criticism and moral superiority come ever so easily. Lionel Trilling has said "our culture peculiarly honors the act of blaming, which it takes as the sign of virtue and intellect." To understand people and to hunt untiringly for matters to praise in them certainly cannot raise wrecks but they do far more to save human beings from drowning then the judgemental approach which costs nothing and is worth about as much. Hostility keeps us defensively locked in some obstinacy we are secretly sick of but cannot surrender until someone assures us we are some good. When that happens, it is remarkable but we seem to be able then to acknowledge that such cheering tribute may well be overgenerous and at the same time really to want to deserve it some day.

A change of mind becomes a possibility when we see the attractiveness of the better way and find ourselves genuinely wanting to walk it. The process is profoundly connected with the mysterious grace of hope, hopefulness about life and oneself. The awakening of hope and spititual desire is in itself a mysterious thing. It is certainly not something one gives to people. It is there, within them, but so often repressed under false hopes and defensive wants and anxiety-rooted expectations. If people can be helped to see the irrelevance and destructiveness of these mistaken strategies and can risk abandoning them, then it seems that hope does "spring eternal," a well of water uncovered and released to spring up within them and refresh and invigorate their life.

The words "penitence" and "repentance" are now rather poor words for this miracle. Their Latin root and subsequent use in Christian spirituality have emphasized the painful and backward-looking aspects of this process. There are no such suggestions in the Greek word used in the New Testament. There the word simply means a change of attitude, a new stance; and that is the essence of the thing. The regret that comes to the mind looking back on its mistakes and misunderstandings has only a limited value. In the true penitence, the genuine fresh start, that mishandling of life actually assumes a kind of grace because it is life now understood. The Eastern Orthodox scholar Evgeny Lampert has written "Repentance is no denial of one's past; on the contrary, it is a moment of initiation by which the past acquires new meaning. . . . The moment the prodigal son fell on his knees and wept he made his past sacred moments in his life."[8]

3

BELONGING

Standing by the cross of Jesus were his mother, and his mother's sister, Mary the wife of Clopas, and Mary Magdalene.

When Jesus saw his mother, and the disciple whom he loved standing near, he said to his mother, "Woman, behold, your son!"

Then he said to the disciple, "Behold, your mother!" And from that hour the disciple took her to his own home.

St. John 19:25-27

THE UNUSUAL LENGTH of the Bible and the bewildering diversity of its contents must be largely responsible for the scarcity of its readers. To open it is to have in one's hands not just a great quantity of words but the life of centuries, so that a great investment of time and deep attention is required from anyone who wants to understand it. But it is generally agreed that to readers who give its study this devotion it appears increasingly to be a whole.

Although written by many hands, certain of its ideas and meanings regularly recur, accumulating significance as the book progresses, so that the full meaning of a passage frequently cannot be discovered in itself but seems to require extensive reference to other parts of the volume.

St. John's gospel has this characteristic feature of the Bible to a remarkable degree. Generations of Christians of course must have read it without the help of commentaries, and their reading was for them the presence of God, but they must have missed much of the magic and mystery of the text as they settled for such moral or merely factual interpretation as they could extract from it. It is when the ambiguity and the buried allusion are made clear, and the Old Testament echo heard, that the surface sense of the words is revealed as a set of clues to a deeper and more fascinating truth.

Accordingly one needs to become accustomed to seeing St. John's writing palimpsestically. Things said and written previously are just visible underneath. Elements of the past are there by implication. This intrinsic potency and resonance of St. John's words may make his meaning elusive but they are part of the unique fascination that his thought and feeling have always held in the Christian world and to some extent outside it as well. The words from the cross "Woman, behold your son" owe their mysterious gravity to an accumulation of meaning characteristic of this gospel.

For Jesus and his contemporaries it was apparently a natural and polite form of speech to address a woman as "woman."

That a son should address his mother in this way was extraordinary and suggests some deliberate formality and solemnity.

The only other incident in this gospel that includes the mother of Jesus is the marriage feast at Cana (St. John 2:1-11). On that occasion Jesus uses the same perplexing formality, addressing his mother as "woman." There is also an unexpected and disconcerting reserve in their relationship, as though her role as mother of Jesus is going to change and St. John wants to suggest even now some anticipatory sense of this coming alteration in what she is for, what her bright meaning is. And there is the idea of a necessary waiting for this until some hour of destiny has struck.

Jesus' "hour," in St. John's understanding of the sinister and glorious story, is the hour of his completed task, when he is lifted up on the cross to show what everything stands for in this world of shifting appearances. Things stand or fall by how they look there, where faith, hope and love "costing not less than everything" will exercise their magnetism to the end of time. If men look long enough at it they may come to see why they are given life.

And as that hour struck, once again Jesus addresses his mother as "woman," but this time without reserve, this time with infinite love because now is the hour for the last arrangement. On the verge and rim of things, with everything done that had to be done save this, he binds her and the disciple he loves in a belonging as profound as birth. "'Woman, behold your son.' Then he said to the disciple 'Behold, your mother.' And from that hour the disciple took her to his own home."

From a very early date Christians have seen the symbolism of this passage and the way the collective voice of the Bible speaks in it as giving it a far weightier meaning than a matter of fact interpretation of it can bear. The loved disciple means more than just himself. He signifies every Christian. In the strange use of the word "woman" for Jesus' mother are haunting resonances of the archetypal Eve in the Genesis creation story, of Israel as the Daughter of Zion, of the woman "robed with the sun, beneath her feet the moon" bringing forth the Messiah and other offspring in Revelation chapter 12.

Moreover, English translations do not make clear that the Greek text of the passage refers twice to Jesus' mother simply as "the mother" and to the disciple whom Jesus loved simply as "the disciple." The two are described by St. John not by their proper names but by their vocations, as belonging now to a new dimension of solemnity, so that they become types, icons, of the mother church and of the disciple-family of Jesus.[1]

In fact, in this image of Jesus completing his work by giving his mother, virtually addressed as the new Eve and the new Israel, and John, the typical Christian, to one another, St. John saw the founding of the Church and the inauguration of the deep relationship between the Church and all generations of believers. The bond between them was first made in pain at the foot of the cross, and re-made in joy three days later. It is from that time and place that the Church, by teaching, fellowship, sacrament and prayer, brings forth and nurtures successive generations of the new Israel, the disciples of Jesus, and makes them a family.

And it is as a representative figure and symbol of the great family of the Church, of the Church militant and triumphant, that the mother of Jesus assumed her new role and meaning obscurely hinted in the story of the marriage at Cana.

She is not the only saint who helps the Christian to lay hold of the mystery of that communion of faith and love in which he meets the conditions of life, enjoys its enjoyments, argues its problems. A few of them have attracted the love of almost the whole Church, and for centuries. Many others have received the thankfulness and affection of small groups who felt drawn to them as spelling out some intriguing or perplexing part of the Christian idea that for personal reasons particularly engaged their attention. But no saint has had so prolonged a role in Christian imagination nor one that has unfolded in such diverse significance as the Blessed Virgin Mary.

Most people at times, and some few people perhaps all the time, want to dispense with images as they think of God in prayer. They may indeed begin with some image and its attendant associations but eventually they find their minds pressing through these or looking over and beyond them in simple desire for God himself who is who he is and has left enough clues of his reality about the world to keep humanity continually wanting more. So, the author of *The Cloud of Unknowing* wrote "Lift up your heart to God with humble love: and mean God himself, and not what you get out of him . . . you find only darkness, and as it were a cloud of unknowing. You don't know what this means except that in your will you feel a simple steadfast intention reaching out towards God . . . I will leave on one side everything I can think, and choose for my love that thing which I cannot think . . . By love he can be caught and held, but by thinking never."[2]

But for most of us it is necessary also that what we think of God, what is rightly to be thought of God, should be focused in an image, to which we return again and again, a kind of landmark in the mind yet not only marking that to which we thankfully return but also causing a stirring and excitement that set up resonances in the mind on many levels.

For the Christian the supreme focus of all that can be rightly thought of God is Christ himself. But there are round him in the Christian imagination subsidiary forms and instances of all that he means, in the shape of sacraments, sacramentals, holy people, holy places, holy times. Indeed there is no reason why the spiritually perceptive mind should not think of everything as in some kind of relationship to Christ, even seeing his blood within the deep vermilion in the rose. In the image of his mother there is a power of vital commination that is unique among created things. It has been part of the Christian joy to discover that much of what Christ signifies seems to have been given to her to carry and represent which otherwise would have eluded the grasp of faith.

In countless churches throughout the world can be seen some representation of this haunting trinity from St. John's gospel, of the crucified savior and at the foot of his cross the mother and the disciple, the point of pain and love at which the church was born.

It is a way of saying a multitude of things; for example, that we are not alone, that Christ has abolished our isolation, and particularly the loneliness of pain. We never pray alone. There is no such thing as private prayer in the sense of solitary prayer. When we pray in the fellowship of the spirit it is always together with the rest of the crowd. We certainly suffer together. We were originally given to one another in the misery and horror of one man's last earthly afternoon. It is part of the prayer of distress to work in to the natural feeling of being quite alone, which pain always rapidly installs in the mind, this faith that we suffer what we have to suffer always within the love and concern of the unseen family.

This part of the work involved in Christian suffering is made harder for many people by their mistaken expectations of the local church and indeed of faith itself. Too often they expect the life of faith to provide answers to their problems as a mother answers a child's questions, and life in the church to differ from life at home or at work by being undisturbed by disappointments, hostilities, failures. These exaggerated expectations may be due to a keen sense of how curiously useless and empty life is without God and to a corresponding but mistaken perfectionism about life with him. The novelist Antonia White, writing of her return to faith after many years of lapse, comments on the way people imagine that faith involves the receipt of complete mental security in exchange for the surrender of intellectual perplexity and the honor of the mind.

> Personally I haven't found it like this at all. On the contrary I am more violently harassed by doubt, insecurity, ambivalence and rebelliousness than ever, and to be once more in St. Peter's boat is to be subject to such violent seasickness that every few months I am tempted to throw myself overboard . . . And frankly

I don't like a lot of the company I find myself in any more than they like me. But that is irrelevant and not a serious difficulty. In fact if the Church is what she claims to be, she *should* be full of the most mixed, incongruous and mutually antipathetic human beings.[3]

The local church acquires an extremely unattractive look if it is loaded with responsibility it cannot bear. It is not the superior character of its fellowship or its admirable service to the community or its elegant liturgical life that make it the holy and oddly enduring realm where faith revives and love is found to be worth believing in. Normally its fellowship is as unsatisfactorily sensitive and peppered with antipathies as human fellowships come, its service to the community is insignificant when compared with such service professionally organized, its worship (apart from the notable centers of praise) oscillates agitatedly between antique and trendy styles as it struggles to hold the attention of the worshippers, occasionally, some think, succeeding. What the believer belongs to in Christ is something that includes all that but is other and greater, a realm visited by grace whenever certain words are spoken in a certain manner, when the water of Christian meaning is poured over new life, when bread and wine in a setting of word and silence make it possible for us to understand what being thankful and being offered can amount to. And in that realm the invisible throng of the dead who saw life in terms of what happened to and through Jesus are always around, the witnesses we cannot see though it is thought they in some sense see us, whose help we cannot fathom but can be content to believe in.

It is possible and common to forget this, but it is also possible to recall it and the way it links the faded past with the perplexing present and the intimidating future, and take heart.

The sufferer needs to recall it. The suffering Church of today, dismayed at the poor impression it makes for God, needs to recall it. Devotion to the mother of the Lord, first and most loved Christ-lover, figure of the Church in God's purpose, is a means and mode of such recall and to that kind of faith and

love in which the blemishes of the Church, its failures and sins
and even the prospect ahead of it, are seen in no way to jeop-
ardize the joy and peace of believing.

Everything in life is small compared with the momentous
item imagination can make of it. Suffering uses the imagination
to magnify its drama and give us a curious exaltation and
depression in being different from others. So doing it deceives
us. In our society far more people are troubled with secret or
confessed unhappiness than are contented with the way things
go. When pain takes over we are unable to see this. The outside
world, as it thrusts itself into our consciousness through the
mass media, shows us our environment as one in which such
terrible things happen and such trivial successes are so enthusiastically applauded that anyone struggling with a private dismay wonders where in this dreadful mixture his alienated self
can possibly fit. It is, moreover, a world in which success carries such prestige that any form of suffering, even misfortune
like physical illness or bereavement, is easily construed as one
of the thousand species of failure. One is vaguely guilty at
feeling low when the world throbs away with the vibration of
so many cheerful people doing each his own robust thing.

This inability to recognize anyone of one's own kind, for all
are strangers, is the essence of loneliness. It is a kind of blind-
ness, because everyone passing us in the street, or drifting by
unresisting on the same wave of impulse-buying through the
supermarket, fears old age, death and even lesser losses, resents part of his life, would like there to be more meaning and
much more tenderness in the world.

But the sufferers' eyes are held so that they do not see the
wounded stranger beside them. There is, consequently, the desire to withdraw. Unable to face any more, they try to put some
distance between themselves and life, partly to avoid the re-
proaches and perhaps even the pity of others, partly to prevent
the exposure of the self to the risk of more hurt. The withdrawal
intensifies and spreads to more situations. The amount of life
we can cope with diminishes. We become dependent on a few

people near us who find us more and more difficult to please or console and themselves become perplexed by the ambivalent emotions aroused in them by their worried obligations towards us.

To withdraw in this way is in fact to turn from the *work* of suffering. When some great loss or reverse radically changes life for us it is absolutely necessary actively to re-negotiate life on a new set of terms. To work through distress successfully is not given to anyone who has written off mankind for whatever reason. We need to remain in the real world where real people are. We may hope that they will help us. We may be garrulous to the point of boring our friends as we rehearse our complaints and fears. They may see clearly that much of our talk is a way of avoiding rather than attending to the matter. Still, if they will keep listening, concealing weariness, they hold us in the real world and save us from being lost in the labyrinth of self-preoccupation.

The Christian's belonging to the Church is not to be defended as providing a form of that social dimension which is necessary to every fully human life. But it is part of the Christian outlook that we come to fulfillment together, do not find life good when too much alone, are meant to belong. It is being argued that the decline of the Church in our time is part of a general breakdown in community and the onset of a massive privatization of life whose sinister reality is not concealed by fashionable criticism of the faults of institutions. The Christian Church may experience much further reduction in numbers, but, however small, it will always express the importance which the believing community has in Christian faith, it will continue to invite individuals into fellowship in Christ, and incidentally give opportunity for that emotional involvement in the world of people (not all by any means chosen to suit one's preferences) which every mature person needs.

The believing community, for the Christian, extends across time as well as space. The living and the departed are forever members of the same family and called to bear each others' burdens, looking to one another for help and companionship. The Orthodox Church has made this aspect of Christian belonging a particularly significant part of its spirituality.

> Because the saints pray for us, it does not follow that they come between us and God. . . . While Christ is the one and only mediator, there is yet a sense in which every Christian is called to be a co-mediator and co-redeemer through and with him. The Christian is saved not in isolation but as a member of the community; he is saved in and through others. We can only be saved when praying for the salvation of all and with the aid of the prayer of all.[4]

Many of us, however, need some finite summary and symbol that will assist our grasp of this infinite mutuality, without confining it though truly giving access to it. The meeting of such need is not confined to religious experience. In many experiences we know that there is much more in that to which we are responding than what we immediately perceive. Our happiness in the company of someone we love is a quite limited appreciation of just those features of the loved presence that are in our awareness at the moment. And yet we believe we have access to the whole of this person's being, and communion with it. The particular focuses an infinite world, too wide and deep for us to comprehend without the representative aspect through which we meet it and know that we meet it.

The Blessed Virgin Mary is the loved image of the vast world of mutual giving and receiving into which we have entered through faith in Christ; she is a living part of it who in being loved and honored gives access to the whole and to all that grace which God has chosen to mediate through the fellowship of the spirit.

One such grace, expressed in her standing at the foot of the cross, is that of remaining with the pain into which life has brought us.

We may not see what good can come of this refusal to turn away and withdraw. The situation may be one of those whose terror is most vivid precisely in the fact that there seems to be nothing we or anyone else can do about it.

But if it is clearly our life's structure just now and we stay with it, living it through, with as little reservation as possible, it does in fact change, it leads into the next situation. That next situation will have some newness which, though small, may make all the difference, brighten the problem with a more manageable look. And we have changed too. We are certainly more used to its presence, a little more familiar with it, a little less daunted by it.

If, on the other hand, we refuse to stay with our assignment, and consciously or unconsciously evade it in some way, we only find that it meets us again later, when we are less able to cope with it. It comes at the wrong time, and we who meet it the second time round know we turned our back on it before and are the less confident for that reason.

For example, working through grief has to be done more or less when the loss strikes. If there is some pretence at being stronger and more imperturbable than one is, or there is some fear of emotional honesty (perhaps because it may reduce us to a mess of tears) it will be found that the work of grieving is postponed, and not only postponed but obscured, hidden somewhere, to become an inward tone of sadness, difficult to understand. It is as though unshed tears become a poison diffused throughout the system, inhibiting our response to life, slowing us down.

Staying with the grim situation is made easier by thinking no further than the next few minutes. If we wonder how we shall stand it for some indefinite period ahead we shall sink. The imaginary burden of the future will overwhelm us. No one is ever asked to bear tomorrow's load today. Today may be just about as much as we can stand. To add to it the imagined feel of tomorrow's demand on us may well finish us. Baron von Hügel advised a friend in distress "to treat the question how we are going to stand this for a month, or a week, or a day, or even an hour, as a little presumption on our part. We cannot really, of ourselves, 'stand' it properly, for half an hour; and God will and does give us His grace to stand it for as long as ever He chooses, provided we will, according to the intensity of the trial, contract our outlook to the day, or the hour, or even the minute. God, the essentially timeless, will thus and then help His poor timeful creature to contract time to a point of most fruitful faith and love."[5]

Suffering is vastly more than enduring. It is a program of action and work. Christians struggling with their prayer of distress have looked again and again at the Blessed Virgin Mary at the foot of the cross and sensed the characteristic pull of faith and love, keeping them in their world of pain, pleading that on no account are they to think they have freedom to leave it for some easier world of escape or contrivance. Her image has also admitted the mind into the kind of work it has to do in suffering.

She taught her son his first preliminary understanding of what is best done when anguish visits us. In the gospels, after the tantalizing shadowiness of his childhood and youth, he suddenly appears again as a grown man, a positive and whole person. Her influence is to be seen in the fact that he clearly has no automatic devices for protecting himself from bruises. He moves with freedom through life, his eyes obviously seeing other things than what is in front of him, fully aware of the realities of each situation, happy or threatening as they are, yet he seems to know that he is doomed. It may be correct to go back to his mother if we want to understand such spontaneity and courage, and try to imagine the way she led him into the world of love and guided his first steps there.

She has a unique place in the Christian understanding of holiness. She carries a marvelous statement of holiness as a trust in and communion with God learned and maintained (like her son's later obedience) through the things one suffers, a belonging to God worked out through the needs and decisions of every day. And this belonging to God is a matter of saying "Be it unto me according to the word" and sustaining all the action that follows from such desire, such commitment.

The action is of two kinds, relative to the double nature of God's will. God's will is, on the one hand, all that *is* at any given moment, in the sense that he permits the existence of the whole state of affairs in which the believer finds himself. It is God's permissive will for every believer at any given moment that he should be alive in that world in those conditions. To say "Be it unto me according to thy word" means, with a dropping of rancor and an assumption of open-armed readiness, to accept the conditions, because it is the will of God, who cannot be other than loving, that one should in fact *be* just now in those circumstances.

God's will is, on the other hand, what he wants us to *do* in this moment, the action or endurance or enjoyment he calls us to offer him in these circumstances. To say "Be it unto me according to thy word" is to accept God's signified will and to set about doing it in faith.

Holiness is this acceptance and action, this accepting and doing the double will of God. It must necessarily be different for every individual. Every believer is in a sense always on his own with God, accepting and doing the will in one unique and unrepeatable situation after another, because it is his life that he is living, not the life of the man next door. We know a few of the doings, enjoyings, sufferings through which it is thought the mother of our Lord worked out what it meant for her to take life according to God's word. It does not matter that we do not know more. It is rather important that there should not be more, because holiness is a journey into the unknown for everyone, for Jesus and his mother and us. We are not given a heroism, a success to carry in the mind as a model; such models can depress as easily as inspire. We are given a posture, an attitude, an openness to life and to the utterly trustworthy Lord and Giver of life—"Be it unto me according to thy word." We cannot know much beforehand what God's word and will may be. We cannot know today what he will say to us next week. All we know is that in every situation he is present, seeking to make clear to us what he wants done with what is happening to us, and offering the grace in which it can be done in that faith, hope and love that are going to remain when everything is done that has to be done.

St. John's vision of the Blessed Virgin Mary as a figure of the Church, the disciple given to her as to a mother, suggests the possibility that the world of the feminine provides significances essential to the unfolding of the Christian religion that are not available in any other dimension of life.

In recent years there has been much discussion about the masculine and the feminine and much criticism of conventional ways of distinguishing them. All seem agreed that the differentiation of the two terms is an exercise of considerable difficulty and endless fascination. One view is that the fundamental difference between the sexes is that man is essentially the *manipulator*, the one who sees the world as material, to be taken, modified if necessary, and used in the interests of some purpose, while woman is essentially *the one who sees the world with concern*, concern for life, for being, for the well-being of what lives, and with a sympathetic sense of the unity and continuity of life.[6] There is a poem of Hugh MacDiarmid, called "The Two Parents" which is concerned with this contrast:

> I love my little son, and yet when he was ill
> I could not confine myself to his bedside.
> I was impatient of his squalid little needs,
> His laboured breathing and the fretful way he cried
> And longed for my wide range of interests again,
> Whereas his mother sank without another care
> To that dread level of nothing but life itself
> And stayed day and night, till he was better, there.
>
> Women may pretend, yet they always dismiss
> Everything but mere being just like this.[7]

No human being is entirely masculine or entirely feminine. Each of us is an androgynous being with our masculine and feminine elements in varying proportions. But if the world is to recover hope and zest for life there must be a nourishing of

the feminine within us and it, a development of sensitive concern, for life, for being, for well-being, to balance the twentieth
century's ruthless manipulation of the world and its contents in
the pursuit of shortsighted aims.

The Church would help this recovery by giving as much
attention to being as it gives currently to doing, by discovering,
perhaps with some excitement, what it now is and has in Christ.
And the individual believer can be part of the desired spiritual
growth as he reflects that the attitude to experience given in the
Mother of God's "Be it unto me according to thy word" involves a view of God as trustworthy, as caring. it is true that
lives fragment, that hearts break, that some suffering seems
unreachable. Still, the movement of life, in the Christian view,
however menacing it looks, is sooner or later seen to be entirely
for us, in the sense of for our growth in faith and love and fullest
joy. It can be trusted to come right in the experience of the
patient, the imaginative, the affectionate. People do not have to
fight it and subdue it. It is enough if they are in communion
with it; then all the larger forms of meaning and hope appear
again.

4

PROTESTING

Now from the sixth hour there was darkness over all the land until the ninth hour.

And about the ninth hour Jesus cried with a loud voice, "Eli, Eli, lama sabachthani?" that is, "My God, my God, why hast thou forsaken me?"

St. Matthew 27:45-46

WE CAN NEVER BE SURE what exactly was the dream and hope, like a flare in his mind's eye, that beckoned Jesus to Jerusalem and death. There is much to be said for the view that he felt himself caught up in a spiritual process that had a momentum of its own, and was gathering pace, as it swept forward to a storm at whose heart would be his faithfulness to what he believed or his betrayal of it. If he was faithful, whatever happened to him God would intervene and bring in his kingdom, and the thrilling light of history's fulfillment would flood the world.

As the darkness deepened that afternoon, and his faithfulness seemed to have amounted to nothing but the ordinary death a million faithless people die, he felt that the thing he had lived with so long, this hope and the presence of God so intimately associated with it, had vanished with the light. In his cry can be heard many human cries, but one of them is the man of faith's most terrible shock and dismay, that he has been wrong all the time.

When the worst comes to the worst and there is the maximum sense of danger, human beings draw on their animal inheritance and they fight or run. The cry of protest, one of the most sincere prayers men every pray, is part of that fight against the unacceptable situation which is the first natural response to it on the part of people of energy and spirit. Inability to believe that the worst has happened struggles with rebellion as the realization that it has in fact happened slowly penetrates the mind. In the life of faith, this tension that forms the initial experience of shock is expressed in the prayer of protest. It is basically a prayer of faith in that it assumes a view of life as reasonable and explicable. There is no point in protest if life is a random and irrational affair or if the present is determined entirely by its physical antecedents. To rail against God has a natural place in the religious life, though it is a preliminary phase that will either reduce faith to a morose hostility to things in general or be absorbed and dispersed in the widening of one's vision as the suffering is worked through.

The Bible is at its most human and believable when its many dismayed and incredulous figures make their protest and put their angry questions to life. This strain of faith appears dramatically in the prophets' loneliness, is marvelously strident in the psalms, and reaches a unique and majestic articulation in the book of Job. It is always a part of sensitive religion.

Many twentieth-century people cannot move beyond the stage of fighting God over the misery and injustice of life. They are misunderstood if they are regarded as unspiritual or unbelievers. They wrestle with life and see it as the resisting stranger; the light has not yet dawned for them in which they see it as the God who blesses.

It is a pity that the prayer of protest, so clear in the Bible and consecrated by the Savior's use of it, is so infrequent in the public prayer of the Church. Through the press, TV and radio people are daily exposed to the unhappiness and despair of the world, the exhaustion and anger in people's hearts, the loneliness and misunderstanding that haunt their personal relationships, and it is natural for them at times to wonder how much longer it has to go on and whether it must in fact always be like this. They think of the great need of the world for peace so that people can be set free to right the terrible imbalance of wealth and opportunity amazed at the incalculable price of suffering that people are having to pay to learn how to create a stable international structure. They observe scientific advances of thrilling ingenuity and beautiful contrivance, and that they have about as much effect on the total evil of the world as the rain on the saltiness of the sea. The angry heart protests. Yet little of this genuine religious emotion is ever expressed in public Christian prayer.

Behind this unwillingness to be honest to God is an unrealistic view of faith as imperturbable and frictionless. It is as unrealistic as that sentimental view of a happy marriage as an uninterrupted harmony in which the sedate partners "never had a cross word in thirty years." The absence of verbal strife does not imply the presence of love or intimacy. Some conflict is a

natural and healthy aspect of intimacy. Its absence in a sup-
posedly ideal marriage could be a sign of positive good but it
could on the other hand be due to a deep fear that the marriage
will not stand the expression of differences or to the fact that
husband and wife are driven by perfectionist interpretations of
Christian love. In either case it is not an authentic love that
presents that serene exterior to the world. Where there is deep
love, in spirit and in truth, husbands and wives are free to be
themselves to one another and can share their negative as well
as their positive feelings. In this sense a certain amount of conflict can be, instead of the sign of waning love it may seem,
one of the many forms of deep mutual involvement and unity.

And the life of faith, if it is genuine and full, will be able to
sustain believers' periodic wish, under the stress of adversity,
to arraign God with the contradictions and intractableness of
human life, allowing them for the health of their souls to turn
distress into prayer and for the time being to reject God in the
bitterness of their hearts.

The common idea in religious circles that a spiritually mature person will always be joyful is absurd. It ignores the fact
that spiritual health provides no immunity to failure, disappointment and the thousand natural shocks that flesh is heir to,
and it seems to assume the desirability of a joy that is independent of the sufferings of mankind as a whole and of the misfor-
tunes of people we love. The truth is that our happiness depends
not only on the firmness of our hold on some chosen set of
values but also on the wellbeing of people we love and the
progress of causes and enterprises with which we have identi-
fied ourselves. Freud's famous remark that the aim of his treat-
ment was to replace neurotic suffering by ordinary unhappiness
may sound gloomy, but behind it is the observed fact that the
suffering of the neurotic often tends to be a rather self-con-
cerned experience, which to some extent actually protects him
from the kinds of pain that inevitably come to people who fully
participate in life and allow its common agonies and aspirations
to pass through them and hurt and inspire them, as indeed they

must if they are truly felt.[1] Freud was virtually saying that to be a healthy person is to be unhappy when unhappiness is appropriate. In the same way, to be a person of authentic Christian faith is to protest when protest is natural. God does not expect us to deny our own truth and suppress our inner revolt against the apparent wrongness of things but to express it in the prayer of the outraged heart.

When this has been done the real work of suffering can begin. Sooner or later, if we are not to disintegrate or live forever with the fountain of life within us poisoned by resentment, we shall want to attempt making some sense of what has happened. Some of its roughness will soften as we see that it is in certain ways like other events which the mind normally accepts. If we are not quite blinded by our own distress we may recall similar trouble happening to others no more deserving of life's sinister side than we. If the situation in no way fits in with our established view of the world we shall need to modify the assumptions and expectations that have formed that view, so that a new self can be built up which functions with greater competence and can sustain and indeed absorb the new situation instead of unrealistically rejecting it. And that in fact is the true work, the essential journey into the interior, to which God calls every sufferer.

All that hurts is not suffering. So pains need to be sifted and classified. A certain amount of pain is one of the ingredients of happiness.

To be engaged in a mode of living that employs the whole of oneself, to be realizing one's aims sufficiently for enthusiasm and interest in life to continue and deepen, to be learning how to get self-regard out of one's attempts at love and compassion—anyone so doing, thinking, feeling, already knows happiness.

If that is so, then wanting, and therefore *not* having, are part of happiness; and so is effort, and effort implies sometimes succeeding and sometimes failing. That is to say, a certain amount of failure and frustration and dissatisfaction and longing and summons to more effort is part of the structure of human joy. That is not suffering, though it often hurts.

And there is a certain pain of the mind that is essential to human dignity. The contentment of the animal, living almost entirely for the moment and the satisfaction of the moment's instinctive need, is not for human beings while they remain truly human. Since they have minds that reflect and enquire they cannot stop themselves examining the human condition, observing what life lacks, acknowledging spiritual greatness in the past and feeling its inspiration, weighing up what disturbs their contemporaries and what they applaud. All this at times uncomfortable concern is part of the full life of human beings with the dignity and honor of the mind. To want to surrender it is to want not to live. It belongs to us as human, as fully participating in life, not to us as suffering.

Deeper still, the capacity to register loneliness and forsakenness is a pre-condition of happiness because it is part of being a real person, an individual. Surrender the space, the distance between you and life and it is impossible to love it, you cannot even know it, you can only merge with it. Each of us reacts to experience with his own modest equipment and in his own awkward way but he becomes a person precisely through registering sharply life's disquieting or exciting events as an affected individual and not with the diluted unselfconscious response of the herd. As the self develops and refines its awareness of life it will often find itself alone. At the heart of our most intense appreciations of the beautiful, our understanding of social good, our experience to personal guilt, longing, disgust at life, thirst for God, there is always a disconcerting solitariness and incommunicability. To mature in the life of faith is to come to terms with this loneliness as one aspect of life's goodness. If we try to deny its existence or seek some warmth of affection or peace that will obliterate it we are on the wrong path, we are really longing for some womb-like state before, by being born, we had this precious, ambiguous gift of individuality bestowed on us.

If we have come to terms with this essential loneliness, and not reluctantly but seeing it as part of the marvelous trouble being human is worth, to be listed thankfully in the inventory of a truly personal existence, we shall be emotionally free to deal with exceptional loneliness thrust upon us by circumstances. That does not mean that we shall never have to sustain overwhelming isolation, never have to cry out with forsakenness like the broken man of the Christian religion. But if we are reconciled to the human condition, to the infinite possibilities of joy and pain that being a self involves, we shall have done the "remote preparation" for the dark hour and shall find that we are open to the grace God offers in it.

Part of the grace offered Jesus was a form of prayer for his pain. He had once spoken about the hour of maximum danger, when all our defences disappear and we are exposed to life's ultimate menace, as one in which it would be given us what to say. What was given him was a religious form for his dismay, a shape of protest and meaning and faith, familiar from his youth but never so needed as now.

The words "My God, my God, why hast thou forsaken me?" are the cry which begins Psalm 22. Someone is suffering, struggling to make sense of it, and continuing to believe. A dramatic psalm, with marked changes of mood, it moves all the way from blaming God, through the re-assertion of faith and the certainty that deliverance will come, to the conviction that ultimately the whole world will acknowledge God's goodness. It is an honest prayer of extraordinary nobility, prayed by one who shared Jesus' religious tradition hundreds of years before, by many other sufferers in the years between, and now by Jesus, as death approached, having to draw for sanity on whatever resources of the spirit he had discovered. One of those resources is the fellowship of the spirit; a man finds it a reality when the words of the common prayer of the community of faith become the voice of his own heart.

Working through suffering involves resisting the contraction of one's world to the single point of pain which is all it seems to be just now. Jesus is shown achieving this resistance, recovering his sense of the whole meaning which his tradition of faith had given to life and its pain, and living this hour through in that meaning, not outside it. In that tradition many people before him had worked through their apprenticeship in suffering and humiliation and argument with God. He drew on it, on all that those men had said, he let the great voice of the religious spirit speak, giving himself to it to speak through; and it is the stronger for us now because it said it all for him then, and enabled faith and love, not meanness and despair, to pour into the world from his death.

In the spiritually of the Bible the whole of life is seen as something given.

> "The given" includes both the good and the evil in (the believer's) life, and it is to this whole life that love of God brings salvation from despair. If God were only relevant to the good in a man's life, He could not bring hope or salvation to it. It is essential for these things to be possible that God loved man *whilst he was yet a sinner.* J. L. Stocks recognized the importance of this truth when he said: "This Love and Wisdom is conceived as the endorsement equally of every feature of the world process, of what seems to us bad as of what we think good. (God is the cause not of all things, but only of the good, said Plato, but wrongly: his God was not a God of love)."[2]

So in the psalm on the lips of Jesus that Friday afternoon

> O my God, I cry by day, but thou dost not answer:
> and by night, but find no rest.
> Yet thou art holy,
> enthroned on the praises of Israel

is heard the authentic utterance of the religious person who knows by faith that helplessness and pain do not mean that God is any less to be trusted (indeed we will the more tenaciously trust). Confidence and joy do not mean that God is any more to be praised (though we may want to give special thanks), that disappointment has no prescriptive right to diminish the amount of love we are willing to offer God, and that death is not terrible when we are reconciled to life. "Yet thou art holy, enthroned on the praises of Israel" is of the same world of thought and experience as Jesus' use of the affectionate word "Father" for him to whom all that happens is ultimately to be referred, even the final darkness to which all that happens seems to come; it is of the same world of thought as Julian of Norwich's "All shall be well, and all manner of things shall be well" and Beethoven's conviction (out of a vast experience of misery) that eternal joy is at the heart of the universe. Faith is getting into that world of thought and staying there as the confirmatory and the challenging signs come and go.

The deep effect Jesus has on us, making our horizon wider, reducing the littleness and the noise, cutting fear down to size, all goes back to what he was. It was not his habit to use prayer as a means of changing God's purpose of his own circumstances. In prayer he was himself before God, expressing the fear or complaint of the moment and letting his mind move on from there, through familiar points in his understanding of providence, until the goodness and holiness of God and life came into focus again. He did not derive his certainty about the holiness of God from the way the world went. It is natural to thank God for events in life that please us and fascinate us, but God is not holy and to be adored because we think that there is a balance of these events over what is unpleasant and devastating. Who has ever done that fantastic arithmetic? To faith God is holy and to be adored whatever happens.

The Christian believes that life is given us for a purpose. There is little sense in seeing that purpose in terms of the quest for personal happiness. One could not imagine a setting in which such a quest would be more doomed to fail for most people than the world we have to live in. But this world is a suitable and indeed hopeful setting for learning faith and love and thankfulness, for finding coherence, for discovering what makes shallow joy and shallow despair look shallow. In such learning and discovering there are moments of deep happiness, but not many serious thinkers claim that continual happiness is available. It has been said that any satisfactory analysis of what it means to have religious faith today will concern three types of experience; they are feeling, loving, and dying.

The most unproductive idea of happiness is curiously enough the commonest. Both flimsy and inflated, it does not represent the fulfillment of any positive goal, only the allaying of anxiety and the compensation of disappointment. Those who carry this ghost in their hearts are doomed to finding reality always falling short of their dream. They must always lose because their wants are never quite reached, are indeed hardly reachable. So life, or life as they imagine it, is always forsaking them. Even if they are lucky enough to find it suddenly coming up to their yearning, their thrill is almost immediately turned into loss by the fear of its not lasting or the suspicion of some hidden imperfection due shortly to come to light.

Secretly their life is driven by the desire to avoid pain. It is being argued today that this is a peculiarly twentieth-century malaise whose result must inevitably be the quick elimination of joy. "Pleasure may be achieved without paying the price of strenuous effort, but joy cannot . . . The progress of technology and pharmacology furthers an increasing intolerance of everything inducing the least displeasure. Thus human beings lose the ability to experience a joy that is only attainalbe through surmounting serious obstacles. The natural waves of joy and sorrow ebb away into an imperceptible oscillation of unutterable boredom."[3] There follows an unnoticed withdrawal from reality, the sentimental recourse to a past that never existed, the longing gaze towards a future that cannot exist, the rejection of the present that does.

To become a real person involves cleaning life's air of all that miasma, asserting the superiority of reality over pleasure, doing what you do as the active center of your life, awakened to intelligent purpose, not as a mere consumer of existence like an infant putting each thing into his mouth. It means relating experience to what one believes about life as a whole, what is worth doing with it and the unavoidable conditions (for example, time and the prospect of death) in which everything that is worth doing has to be done.

Another way of looking at the conditions is to see them as the form of life's continuous creativeness. One such condition is the mutual involvement of change, loss, and gain. It is so all-pervading and universal that it amounts to life's atmosphere. There is no other air to breathe; but it is a good air, the air of life, and those who breathe it deeply know that the last word is always with life.

All suffering is change that is felt to be simply loss—of someone or something considered necessary to life, and so loss that is resented and rejected. The work of suffering involves drawing on one's inner resources to find the ability to let go what life has taken, to accept the change made by its absence, and to achieve a new position from which life continues to be possible. The result of this work is the growth of the spirit, which we believe is a large amount of what living is for. The person who is unable to do the work of negotiating loss and change and finally gaining some fresh or deeper sense of life's meaning must be thought not to have been truly living before, only to have been kept going by a set of circumstances.

Every one of us is continually in one way or another the scene of these two situations, "living and partly living," living and being kept going. Jesus was all living. He was himself the source of his life's meaning and movement. What he set out to give men and women was the power to choose to live, and in the way one's deepest self wishes to live. He wanted them to be free from the need to be kept going by this and that, free because their passion and life would be an inner spiritual fountain not a dependence on the world.

Our first experiences of being forsaken by what is dear to us occur in earliest infancy when we are ill equipped for dealing with them and so are naturally overwhelmed. Each later loss is added to the accumulation of loss experience that began in infancy and perhaps receives some intensification of its bite from those long ago pains. In unhappiness we easily become children again, seeing current loss as inconsolable, forgetting that years of adult experience have widened our life to include now many sources of possible good. Prayer is for realizing this life-enhancing grace of our providential course, for avoiding becoming so obsessed with seeking what is lost that we cannot see what we have and may yet have, and for helping us recover when this crippling myopia comes over us.

To help us come through into the light our prayer must be more than a protest. It must indeed be that, and for as long as a groan is left, but the usefulness of protest eventually wears out. There is a limit to the natural resentment we need to express about any particular injury or ill-luck. When that is reached, if we continue our arraignment of the world, that hostility is obviously being fed by other reasons for disliking existence, or else we are using moroseness as a drug.

There are other forms into which the prayer of protest can productively move. One is the prayer that satisfies the sufferer's deep need for the experience of fraternity, for some human recognition that his tears and arguments are justifiable, that meaning can suddenly vanish for others too. Certain prayers have continually done this for Christians. The Rosary and the Angelus present the anguished with the possibility of understanding their pain and the new responsibility that has suddenly been announced in their life in the drama of another human being's experience.

Veneration of the Blessed Virgin Mary has made accessible to Christians a remarkable world of love and prayer in which sadness can be bathed in genuine emotion and at the same time can be rescued from the sentimentality or indulgence that make it a huge waste. When their distress is mirrored in the life of the mother of Jesus it becomes something they can begin to look at, and so begin to understand, and in terms of Christian faith. To look, to understand, to adore is the whole exercise; it is to come through, to have done the work, to find the peace which Jesus mysteriously said he had left with us. But it begins with being able to look, to face things. The novelist Colette once advised a young writer: "Look for a long time at what pleases you, and longer still at what pains you." An admirer of her work has commented "when we, in turn, watch Colette watching, we realize that, along with love and work, this is the third great salvation, or form of prayer, which we have been given. For whenever someone is seriously watching, a form of his lost innocence is restored. It will not last, but during those minutes his self-consciousness is relieved. He is less corrupt. He forgets he is going to die. He is very close to that state of grace for which Colette reserved the word 'pure.'"[4]

The remaining work, and it is the principal work, of the prayer of distress is to set one's suffering in that wide perspective which is the purpose and promise of God as marvelously explained to us by Jesus. The Eucharist carries a remarkable power to help us do this, its whole motion being towards saving us from ourselves and opening our imaginations to all that is beyond our fears and resentments, to God and the world and the endless goodness and perplexity of things. Revisions of the liturgy that contract its classical dimensions to the intimate and homely do nothing but rob us of the chance of seeing God's glory. It is just one of those things that when our hearts are heavy it is the transcendent, the numinous, the universal that can lift us from the dark rut we are plodding to that spiritual height from which God's meaning may conceivably come into view.

The words and action of the Eucharist enclose a pattern of experience which irradiates life with meaning whatever the worshipper's mood; but when, through deprivation or wound, someone is needing to get used to, and so assert some control over, the unfamiliar and menacing world his life has just become, the Eucharist is a marvelous rescuer from the pit the self is inclined to dig for itself. An offered life culminating in a forsakenness likewise offered is proclaimed as bringing reconciliation of enmities and forgiveness of sins to the world. There is gratitude for that and for every other sign of good which in our preoccupation we may have ignored. There is the rehearsal of other men's needs and pains and what must be done if compassion is to remain alive in this world. And there is the giving of ourselves to that power that will make our gift, mediocre or stricken as it may be, part of the great reconciliation and forgiveness that is the true life of humanity.

To do this serious thing with our suffering is to set it in the largest meaning we know. We shall not succeed at once. It will take considerable time. The work will need to be done over and over again, in Eucharist after Eucharist, that efficacious repetition which Christians were told to use by him who taught them all they know about prayer. But gradually, by this and other means, Christian meaning is worked into our experience; our suffering is annexed to all the believing, hoping, loving that constitute the Lord's body in the world of time.

The hard work of suffering is done when it is irradiated with meaning. Faith's aim is to take this enlightenment through the whole of one's life with its occasional sense of the divine, its shudder at the passage of beauty, its dismay at the accumulation of failures that greets the backward look. If people can find meaning of sufficient dignity in what they do and endure there is nothing they may not eventually call good. Life without meaning, on the other hand, has to be lived in such a curiously superficial way that few people manage it with any success. Those who do enjoy and bear with such a life provoke the kind of amazement set up in the mind by the sight of blind children happy together without the assistance of light.

In the second part of T. S. Eliot's poem ''The Dry Salvages'' he refers to our occasional moments of illumination when everything seems to come together in the mind and life impresses us as being no longer a time-ridden wastage but an eternal whole. As we grow older and these moments of illumination accumulate they gather a certain authority. It becomes possible to think of them not as curious exceptions but as moments when the truth of life becomes clear. Then we realize that most of the time we simply experience life in an uncomprehending fashion; we miss the meaning.

Christian prayer involves in various ways our making repeated approaches to the meaning of life as Jesus lived it. As our hold on the meaning becomes firmer and broader, through worship, prayer, thinking things through, we discover that our bright experiences of life's goodness seem to lose their pastness, they are to some extent restored to us because they take their place now in the continuing whole we see life to be.

> We had the experience but missed the meaning,
> And approach to the meaning restores the experience
> In a different form, beyond any meaning
> We can assign to happiness.[5]

That is to say, our past happinesses are not merely restored to us. They are transformed and deepened. All our past is so transformed, not only its moments of happiness but its sufferings and failures too and indeed the entire past of the physical universe, by being seen as part of that whole which in all its parts carries God's purpose of love, from the sunken life of great oceans to the remotest limits of the stars, from the elusive beginnings of matter to the glory that is man when reason and love articulate through him. The past, our past, is given back to us "in a different form" when so considered because it is seen more profoundly and religiously than the usual meanings which we assign to happiness and pain can express. In faith's wide and trusting vision we begin to see how much deserves to be taken into account. All our first estimates and judgements of our experiences have to be revised.

Of course, when we try to understand what has happened to us and relate it to other aspects of life that have never perplexed us but encouraged and delighted us, believing that the whole should have its ample say as well as the bitter fraction, there is a limit to the exercise. We cannot literally take the whole into account, because we cannot comprehend a whole of which we are part. But we believe that all that exists and happens is penetrated by God's meaning, means some aspect of God's desire

and purpose that we shall come of our own free choice to know
and love him. Not all that happens carries this meaning equally
clearly. In some events it seems to be entirely absent, and if we
are drawn into their dread we shall cry out in anguish and dismay.

Yet our anguish and dismay at the seeming absence of God,
if honest and at the same time purified of mere self-preoccupation, if ready to join compassionately with all who for whatever reason feel forsaken, can turn that pain into a form and
presence of the divine pity.

5

WANTING

After this Jesus, knowing that all was now finished, said (to fulfill the scripture), "I thirst."

A bowl full of vinegar stood there; so they put a sponge full of the vinegar on hyssop and held it to his mouth.

St. John 19:28-29

ST. JOHN SAYS that it was "after this" and "knowing that all was now finished" that Jesus said "I thirst." This must mean that some last thing had just been done in which, almost as death was reaching him, Jesus met the terms of his contract, as he understood the deep agreement between himself and God that began on Jordan's banks when John the Baptist poured the water of meaning over his excited head.

This last thing Jesus had to do, as we have seen, concerned his mother and the disciple he loved:

> When Jesus saw his mother, and the disciple whom he loved standing near, he said to his mother, "Woman, behold your son!" Then he said to the disciple, "Behold your mother!" And from that hour the disciple took her to his own home. After this Jesus, knowing that all was now finished, said (to fulfill the scripture) "I thirst."

We know that the early church very soon began to see a special radiance round the mother of Jesus as in the common mind she became the focus and image of much Christian experience and conviction. In this brief but intense incident St. John sees Mary at the foot of the cross as a symbol of the Church, and the loved disciple as representing the Christian. In these two, church and believer, brought solemnly together by the word of Jesus, can be seen the inauguration of that common life of love and trust in which all Jesus' followers can live after he has died.

And in that common realm of mutual love and shared search into life's truth the successive generations of Christian believers have in fact lived. Established by the word of Jesus, its starting point the foot of the cross, it has often seemed ready to disintegrate but has been held together by the spirit that proceeds from him and the Father. The new Eve, who brings forth and cares for the many brethren of the first born, has continually been threatened, but the Christian mind has clung persistently to a mysterious inner knowledge that the gates of hell will not prevail against her though they may clang with a dead sound on everything else.

The beginning of the church was the last thing Jesus had to do, thinks St. John. That being done, all now being done that was in the mind of God for this chosen person, he says "I thirst." St. John introduced this saying with such solemnity that one is compelled to understand it in the deepest possible way, as an expression of that consuming want which burned continually in all Jesus said and did. In the previous chapter he tells of how, when Jesus was arrested, Peter tried to defend him, and Jesus said to Peter "Put your sword in its sheath. Shall I not drink the cup which the Father has given me?" The cup was the whole life he had sought to live, daily doing the will of God as signified moment by moment, and enjoying or enduring each experience life brought him when lived in this way.

It was Jesus' view that everything, whatever its obvious beauty or pain, is a sign of something else. In all earth's voices another voice speaks. He lived daily in the closest commitment to the world, turning his full gaze in sensitive love and interest on each person who spoke to him, but always listening in depth, alert to the word of God in the word of man. The tremendous mystery of each word that proceeded from the mouth of God increasingly fascinated him and became the driving thirst of his being.

St. John thinks of him, now that all is done that needed to be done, wishing to empty the cup of life of its last drops, in a profound impatience wanting to leave the world he knew for the greater knowing at last within his grasp.

All of us occasionally know this thirst and how life distracts us from it. The truly religious person knows it with such a keenness and persistence that all that the world offers seems bitterness, or at best a cheap satisfaction, when compared with what the heart longs for that is awakened "with the drawing of this love and the voice of this calling."[1] All four gospels say that Jesus was offered sour wine as he died. Perhaps St. John alone saw the irony and anguish in this offering to the man who wants God.

It has often occurred to Christians that Jesus, the supreme example of the person who wants God, is nevertheless in fact every person. This must indeed be the case if Jesus is the image of a human being functioning in that wholeness and freedom for which we were created. It may be argued that everyone, despite appearances, really wants God, and wants him as Jesus wanted him. Even sinful action can be seen as the misunderstood and distracted search for God. All are seeking the one who called them into being, but they weaken and settle for less, through tiredness or ignorance or immaturity. That is to say, they lack energy to reflect on their lives and discover their genuine desires, or they have repressed important areas of themselves and do not now know how much they desire beauty, how much they long for meaning, or they have not grown up sufficiently to be ready to wait, to defer the satisfaction of short-term desires so that long-term wants can have their chance.

Yet the great thirst of human being is for God. The evidence for this is the insatiable quality of human wanting. We have dreams nobler than any tangible forms that we ever have the luck to find, longings charged with more emotion than the satisfactions life gives us can really justify. As long as we have the courage not to call off our hopes, not to mutilate the desiring self, we shall thirst again and again (as Jesus warned) however many and absorbing life's answers and fulfillments. And this curiously haunted character of human experience becomes a "signal of transcendence," a pointer to the supernatural. It is as reasonable to suppose that there is a reality to satisfy our infinite wanting as that we have evolved as creatures whose wants are unaccountably too big for our environment.

The difficulty of explaining this thirst is no reason for not acknowledging it or for assuming that we must have misunderstood it. The religious person is content to feel it and to enquire of life whether there are other impressions of eternity that fit in with it. Thomas Traherne radiates this content in a pervasive happiness that makes him an extremely engaging spiritual writer:

We love we know not what, and therefore everything allures us . . . there is in us a world of Love to somewhat, though we know not what in the world that should be. There are invisible ways of conveyance by which some great thing doth touch our souls, and by which we tend to it. Do you not feel yourself drawn with the expectation and desire of some Great Thing?[2]

On the other hand, if one is unable to interpret this thirst positively it can be a perplexing and even tragic presence in one's life. So Bertrand Russell wrote:

The centre of me is always and eternally a terrible pain. A curious wild pain—a searching for something beyond what the world contains, something transfigured and infinite—the beautiful vision—God. I do not find it, I do not think it is to be found—but the love of it is my life—it's the passionate love for a ghost.[3]

We shall never understand ourselves without becoming quite familiar with the world of our wanting, but we can never know it all. It is possible that the strongest thirst of our being is still unrecognized, still hiding under this and that. Discovering it is a moment of truth at which most people arrive with difficulty though occasionally by some extraordinary grace it is an unexpected gift. Our laziness would sooner accept the wants urged on us by the world's hidden persuaders, deluding us with the idea that we have chosen them ourselves, than examine and sift our values; but we pay a high price for this inertia, in ignorance of true joy and grief, in loss of life-enhancing interest in who we are. Self-interest, self-concern, in the sense of attempting to know oneself and meet its needs, is part of the work of the spiritual life. It is all too frequently repudiated by the clumsy employment of the idea of selfishness—a not very useful term on the whole except as a blunt instrument in judgemental hands.

The pointers to one's true self appear mostly in stillness and quiet. They emerge usually when the attention is relaxed, in marginal and undefined experiences which frequently vanish before recognition but not without leaving a disturbance of mysterious joy. So that alertness and openness are also required, and a willingness to look carefully at all one's experience, with interest but without desire to judge or change it yet, simply ready to know it all as much as it can be known. At some point in all this relaxed waiting, looking, listening, the face of one's love will appear. It is a good sign in the spiritual life of our time that there is so much interest in prayer of the meditative and contemplative kind; it is not only the surest way to God, it is a way of stilling the self, dropping the anchor of one's being and bringing intellect and purpose to rest so that contact is made with the truth of one's depth.

Though we live much of life superficially, knowing only part of who we are and what we want, there is rarely a complete loss of contact with our inner self. There is a hidden light in the fact that our mental life is full of images of things that stand for other things. Our everyday wants are frequently the expression of much deeper needs, but it is a distorted expression requiring decoding and interpretation like the images of a dream. This principle operates on a wide scale.

The twentieth century is not on easy terms with itself. It has great difficulty in finding adequate images for its aesthetic and religious imagination to feed on, it seems unable to conceive purposes worthy of its great vitality and knowledge. Its restlessness appears with notable extravagance in the world of buying and selling. However, the passionate desire to buy and possess more and more new things is perhaps not an example of the materialism so often castigated from the pulpit but essentially a spiritual matter. The primary motive may be not the enjoyment of the new thing but the desire to be rid of the old and too familiar thing, the need to expel what is felt to be used and impure and really so much waste. Things stand for other things. It is not impossible that some deep desire for cleansing, even some obscure cry for forgiveness and new life, struggles to express itself in these remote and uncongenial forms.

When we discover what we really want and can organize our life in that direction, the power of substitute and symbolized wants diminishes. The correction of materialism, as that of "selfishness," is not a matter of direct attack. It is a discovery and exploration of that for which a consumer society is really hungry and thirsty while ignorantly and in unconscious despair it tries to make do with things and money. In a similar way, compulsive eaters (a focus of popular concern significant enough to stand for much in society) need not just to attend to their intake but to know what food means for them particularly, the dissatisfactions they seek to allay through it, the assurance and relationship they achieve in this way. They will discover how much of themselves is involved, the strong emotional link with their earliest solaces in infancy, the loneliness that is both compensated and unfortunately reinforced in this way of consuming life, and the better strategy of a closer association with life so that they can love it and give to it. Things symbolize other things; but the world of hunger and thirst contains so much significance of wanting that again and again the trivial and the important are found to be surprisingly connected.

This is how Simone Weil understands the prayer "Give us this day our daily bread":

> If our energy is not daily renewed, we become feeble and incapable of movement. Besides actual food, in the literal sense of the word, all incentives are sources of energy for us. Money, ambition, consideration, decorations, celebrity, power, our loved ones, everything which puts into us the capacity for action is like bread. If any one of these attachments penetrates deeply enough into us to reach the vital roots of our carnal existence, its loss may break us and even cause our death. That is called dying of love. It is like dying of hunger. All these objects of attachment go together with food, in the ordinary sense of the word, to make up the daily bread of this world. It depends entirely on circumstances whether we have it or not. We should ask nothing with regard to circumstances unless it be that they may conform to the will of God. We should not ask for earthly bread.
>
> There is a transcendent energy whose source is heaven, and this flows into us as soon as we wish for it. It is a real energy; it performs actions through the agency of our souls and of our bodies. We should ask for this food. At the moment of asking,

and by the very fact that we ask for it, we know that God will give it to us.[4]

According to this deep understanding of life, the great hunger and thirst of our being is for the heavenly energy that is love to pour through our minds and bodies, so that the understanding and tenderness and reconciliation of which the kingdom of God is made may come into the world. This is certainly how Christians have traditionally understood this clause in the Lord's Prayer. There have been and still are millions of people, of many religions and none, who think that this is something like the truth about human wanting. They see too that most of the wrongness of life is due to our not wanting love enough, due to our losing heart and settling for less, for what is, however fashionable, a wretched stand-in for love.

We settle for less because deep within us is a fear of growing up to the stature of the fullness of love. In our make-up there is a considerable percentage of both childish indolence and childish haste. They operate to keep us ignorant of our true self, our real desires, and to keep us from the work involved in growing. The indolence is the unwillingness to reflect on our experience, find out what is and what is not satisfying us, and take such action as will diminish resentment and increase the amount of our joy. It is a shrinking from taking active responsibility for our delight in life, from realizing that happiness is a serious business.

Childish haste works in a similar way. To be unable to defer a satisfaction so that one can find out whether it will in fact give what it seems to promise, to be unwilling to interpose some meditating between impulse and act, is a sign of normality in a child but of immaturity in an adult. As with indolence, it seems to be motivated by an obscure fear of life, of the truth about ourselves. To reflect on our intention may reveal the wisdom of modifying it and so provoke disappointment and anxiety. Consideration of this distress may expose the insecurity that would have been allayed by the impulsive action. In this way we are given an indication of the need for some reorganization of the way we go about life. The haste to express the impulse succeeds in preventing such adult reflection by leaving us no time for it.

The indolence and the compulsiveness combine to keep us ignorant of our deep self, unaware of how much it wants to be able to love and would be willing to work for its growth in adult loving. So we live with only half of what there is to us, making do with unsatisfactory fumbling with life's surface, with borrowed goals and substitutes for God. Consequently some of our sufferings are creations of our own; somewhere on them our own fingerprints can be detected. We make the kind of mistakes that people make who must not see some things about themselves that are quite easily seen by others who manage to live not so far from themselves and nearer to the facts.

We make obvious mistakes of over-confidence and self-assertion in order to avoid catching sight of the failure our lost battles have made us think we are; and yet that sensitiveness to humiliation, worked into a different, less evasive way of coping with life, would become a positive asset.

And there are whole tracts of intriguing experience we dare not enter. For example, every so often some aesthetic or religious feelings set off an awakening sound in a neglected region of the mind; but we cannot attend to it because if we did our chosen image of ourselves would begin to shake on its pedestal.

If we have spent any time in the Christian tradition, we are not left alone with these mistakes. The image of a completely whole man, able to respond with all there is of him to all that touches him, is with us for good. By some persisting mercy we are not allowed to forget Jesus. Our thoughts flow indulgently or morosely on, avoiding seriousness, and suddenly he is there, like someone appearing at your elbow. Once we have heard his words, they go on living within us, perhaps a not very robust kind of life, but they are there, giving off light all the time. Through our concealed sadnesses his truth intermittently shines, a cheering glow of meaning, that life being unbeatable had

better be joined and what joining it may mean. Certain possibilities emerge, of reducing our demands, questioning our fears,
discovering that what we thought were liabilities to be ashamed
of may very likely turn out to be valued equipment if we can
switch from fearing life to loving it.

Jesus saw things clearly and ambiguously at the same time.
The more exact he was the more fluid a matter of discussion
became. In the good Samaritan story,[5] the lawyer, himself a
man trained to see issues precisely, is honestly concerned about
the moral uncertainties of the time and particularly about tra-
ditional standards of personal relationships. Jesus neither preaches
nor informs. He confronts this legal man with what he knows
already about the good life, and then he takes him much deeper
to see what genuinely, emotionally, affects him and stirs his
heart—the sight of mercy. He had forgotten that he had that
kind of a heart. He worked daily in a mental world dominated
by the view that life must be controlled by principle and regu-
lation or else it will unravel in disorder, yet all the time his
repressed longing for spontaneity and love to light up the world
was waiting for someone to give it the chance and the courage
to confess itself. If he takes his hand off that heart and lets it
beat freely, life has so much good to give him that many of his
perplexities will seem much more tractable.

The need is for reflection, to discover what we really want
and believe in, what we deeply wish to see and to ally ourselves
with in this shallow time into which God has summoned us.
And this can happen only if we learn to wait and be still, the
mind acquiring the ability to swing between meditation and
contemplation, so that what is beneath the general run of our
thoughts can come to the surface. It is a situation in which the
children of this world are so wide of the mark that their language is quite useful if completely reversed. Put some waiting
into your wanting. That will give you access to the deeper levels
of your being where your own truth and energy and love lie as
yet unused.

To know those wants whose roots go deepest into one's being, to try to give them a more commanding place in one's life, to sense a certain rightness in life as a result of this—and some excitement as well, because life appears now to be opening and unfolding marvelously—many people would say that, while seeing the attraction of such a life style, they could not recognize themselves in it.

For them life is a more disconnected, less coherent affair; they may now be middle-aged but they still find themselves something of an enigma and are continually surprised, sometimes dismayed, at the thoughts that arise in them; they see that growth in love is the point of life and its unqualified good, but they weaken and lose heart if they attempt the formidable task of sorting themselves out. And what bits of philosophy they ever had are blown to the winds when life is stormed by some great complication or loss.

The truth is that much of the time every life is a collection of fragments. Wholeness is always something we are working towards rather than grasping. But some of the fragments are in fact enjoyments, and some are duties and difficulties that are not depressing at all though they may demand much from us. It unifies those bits at any rate to attach as many fragments as we can to such conviction of life's goodness and value as our mind has formed, blessing the name that is above but includes every name of good for our creation, preservation and all the blessings of this life.

In the great complication of grief, only the saint can "see life steadily and see it whole." We shall succumb to seeing it most of the time as reduced to this dreadful fraction of all that is going on. Even so, meaning need not drain away. There is a better and a worse way of living with disaster. However great the good of which life has been robbed by it, new good immediately begins to be made if we choose the better way. There are powerful kinds of good that can come into life only where something has gone terribly wrong. That does not justify even the smallest area of life going wrong; it just happens to be one aspect of the composition of things. There is an Old Testament prayer, "it is good for me that I have been in trouble, that I may learn thy law." There is more in it than that our mistakes at any rate serve to point out and underline the right way. The writer may have discovered this subtle principle of our emotional and spiritual life—the curious bonus attached to good that is erected forthwith on the actual site of failure and loss.

However loose and disconnected life may seem there is good in it that we have known and still know, good that upholds us and excites our admiration and faith. More good will become clear to us if we are willing to give time and thought to understanding such good as has already fallen into our lap from God knows where. The next step is to simplify our lives around such good so that its presence and grace will have room to grow. We can live with dignity only if we live on a few things, chosen for the way they speak deeply to us. We cannot live at all if we do not select from the plenitude of possible experience. We are simply distracted by the meaningless shouts, whispers, pulls, wounds, nudges that time is if human reason and spirituality fail to get to work on it.

The faculty of selection grows more sensitive with use and eventually knows with some certainty what to pick out from our packed time and affirm as sacred. It comes to see that we can be sure of only two moments, the present one and our last. Others may or may not come to us, but this one we now have, and we know that we shall die. "Holy Mary, mother of God, pray for us sinners now and at the hour of our death." The prayer reminds us of the Christian simplification of time, the reduction of that vast problem to the sacred present and eternity. God wishes human beings to be "continually concerned either with eternity (which means being concerned with Him) or with the Present—either meditating on their eternal union with, or separation from, Himself, or else obeying the present voice of conscience, bearing the present cross, receiving the present grace, giving thanks for the present pleasure."[6]

If existence could be simplified as radically as that, its huge disorderly bulk pared down to this moment of love or devastation or beauty or work—and God, our wanting would be simpler, and more vivid for that, but less anxious. Once the center is established, the desire to know God and do his will in and with what is on us now, the rest of our desires lose none of their excitement, only their insistence. None of them has any absolute authority in a committed heart. All are relative, are possibilities only, are subject to time and accident, are changing scenes in which we play the one role of inheritor of life. Consequently we can have as many of them as we wish, will indeed have a great number, as everyone does who finds life interesting. The more we have the better. The less we have the worse it is for us when one of them is suddenly blocked.

The person whose wanting is satisfied in a small area of life, and so confined to that, must suffer terribly if that realm of desire should fall in. It is part of the life of faith to glorify God the creator by enjoying his world, by having many things we like doing, particularly by having time for people. God has made human beings as fascinating and responsive as they are so that knowing and understanding them should be the profound mutuality that it is, a giving that evokes giving, a type of atonement. If emotion is invested in as much of life as possible we shall not turn against life when one form of wanting and enjoying has to change. The part of our life that is joy will come to the help of the part of our life that is grief.

It will certainly need help. The loss of any significant love does not mean that our emotion automatically detaches itself from what we loved. It remains attached to what is now absent and unable to respond in the old way, so that a part of one's innermost self seems to have gone and to belong nowhere. In the anxiety and depression that ensue, our yearning is not only for the lost love but for this part of oneself that is with him or her. Yearning and sadness are forms of wanting that are natural and absolutely right for the experience of loss.

But forms of loving and wanting easily date. The more suitable they were in the original situation the more unwilling we are to change them. But if they do not move and change they become inappropriate to life, which is continually changing. Our emotional response to a loved one present is not appropriate to that loved one absent; its wanting and enjoying need to be changed to the sort of loving that goes with the new situation. Our anxiety and depression and resentment in the experience is over; they belong to an earlier time and are now out of date. Bereavement provokes its appropriate grief and despair. There is a sense in which they are God-given, part of what it is to be a human being; and they have a mercifully protective function in that they provide time for our gradual realization of what has happened before the real work of suffering has to begin. But that situation passes and gives way to a new one, that of having to live and work without the loved person's physical presence. For that demanding task grief and despair are no use at all. They are simply two additional burdens. Not that it is easy to drop them. But it is some little help to know why it is so difficult to get our release. The strength of their hold on us is partly due to the fact that their intense rightness in the original situation has given them a momentum of their own and partly to its being fed by our desire to postpone coping with the new situation. Coping with it can certainly be postponed, but it cannot be postponed itself, because it is here. The new situation is reality.

The attempt to live with thoughts, wants, feelings of another day must dissatisfy us because it is to turn the light of our wanting on the unreal; and it is bound to make a ghost of us. The past draws us because it is known; the bereft present is unfamiliar and seems empty. Yet the truth is that it is the past that is now empty because life has left it, while the present for all its strangeness contains God's kingdom of life and truth. In that kingdom we have our lost loves as God wishes us to have them, as part of our spiritual life. They are living in that dimension of God's love in which flesh and blood are transcended and, precisely because of that, communion with us is possible in the fellowship of the spirit.

In the New Testament account of Easter Day Jesus is described meeting a woman who loved him. As she ran forward to embrace him he told her not to touch him. That is to say, that mode of loving was over; for the two of them it was a thing of death and the past. But a new world of loving was opening before them, with its own language to be learned, its waiting trust and tremendous hope.

At the beginning of great loss such a prospect looks like nothing less than the relinquishing of all that matters. But when the work of suffering is undertaken in faith, it is gradually realized that all God wishes us to relinquish is the past, simply because it is past. The grief-obsessed who cling to the past must inevitably lose all, their love included. To suffer in faith is to allow the past to be the past but to keep hold of the loved one with a brave fidelity in the unfamiliar grasp of faith. To welcome our lost loves into our spiritual present in this way must at first be a hesitating and nervous act of faith for us, but before long they are again part of our current life, in a new form. Someone has called bereavement "loving in a new key."

There is a not uncommon experience that should be connected closely with this kind of loss. When we are quite relaxed, not wanting anything other than the content of the present moment, our mind quite open and ready to receive, there comes to us quite frequently an awareness of the wholeness of life that is profoundly satisfying and reassuring. It comes in a variety of ways and seems particularly associated with the sense of hearing and the sense of smell, though in a very famous example it came through the sense of taste—in Proust's moment of illumination as he tasted a madeleine cake dipped in tea. A passage from well-known and much loved music, the scent of a particular flower briefly brought to us in the motion of the clean air in a summer garden after rain, can evoke the past in a way that is curiously exciting.

It is exciting for two reasons. One is that it is so vivid. It seems to involve more than just remembering the past, which often has an element of mistiness and incompleteness about it. The quality of this experience is its breath-taking sense of reality.

The other is that, unlike remembering, there is no sadness in it, nothing of Tennyson's "so sad, so strange, the days that are no more." On the contrary, it is a joyful and reassuring experience, as though the past is in some sense still alive and has been if only briefly, fused with the present in this moment of communion in depth.

One other feature of this experience of time transcended adds much to its excitement. It has unmistakably that character which Christians call "grace" in that we cannot make it come or persuade it to come by deliberately recalling the past. It is always given, mysteriously and unexpectedly, by some unseen kindness at the heart of life.

We can, however, prepare ourselves for this experience even if we cannot produce it. In the contemplative tradition of Christian prayer the advice has persistently been given to cultivate a simple attention to God or to some aspect of his creation, wanting nothing for oneself, the mind at ease in appreciative openness. It seems that to people who have acquired this inner stillness and undemanding openness, whether within or outside the Christian tradition, who are able to switch off the wanting, planning, selecting mind but leave their love free to be itself, there comes at times this enlightening certainty that life is a unity and that no good is ever lost.

The relaxation of the narrowly wanting mind is at the center of this receptive condition. Joanna Field, in a fascinating exploration of her own route to happiness, says:

> When going my ways with contracted body and narrow focused mind I always felt I was missing things, a feeling of the glory that had departed or that belonged to someone else. Spring was never what it used to be; if only I were somewhere else perhaps it would be better; and I would plunge into aching envy of others who were where I would like to be. . . . But whenever

I could remember to relax, then the glory of my childhood had
not departed, time and place did not matter any more, one sniff
of the morning air brought the distilled essence of all my springs.[7]

In this quest for a stiller heart, for less of the insistent but
unregulated wanting with which our century torments itself,
the Christian has a good start if he will try exploring the belief
in eternal life that has so long been missing from Christian
prayer and conversation.

It may be true that "neither the sun nor death can be looked
at with a steady eye"[8] but so many forms of death and deadness
are with us now that we cannot go on not looking at the subject.
Albert Camus said that to fight against death amounts to claim-
ing that life has a meaning. To Christian believers the life of
Jesus was a continual fight against death and for meaning, and
for the great meaning that both awes and intrigues. We all know
that many short-term meanings can be put into each returning
day as we do this and that as well and as jubilantly as we can.
But that is not enough and it may well be just a way of not
looking at the full glare of death. The deepest thirst of man's
being, however fashionable it is to distrust it, is that life shall
be seen to be honored with significance that includes death, and
indeed all the other losses and deprivations that are minor ver-
sions of death, but in particular death itself, our death, and the
great pile of dead behind us that seem to have been necessary
for us simply to exist at all.

It is not that we dream of some far heaven where on our
arrival God will make amends for all our prefatory pains en
route. We are concerned with a much larger matter and meaning that will give reason and honor to life now, universal life,
from the withdrawn mystery silently continuing in the depths
of the great oceans to what goes on at the last limits of the stars.
It is in the light of great meaning and faith that Christians have
always tried to understand existence and to work meaning into
and out of their sufferings and the world's. People who believe
that death is part of God's purpose, one of the forms of his

caring, can take their time over life. There being a message of beginning or deepening in every ending, their sufferings are worth working through with considerable care. They are not going to miss or lose anything that matters. And there is never any reason for ceasing to love, even for loving less, since every moment, every experience, brings God with it and the possibility of deeper communion with life.

6

ACHIEVING

When Jesus had received the vinegar, he
said, "It is finished"; and he bowed his
head and gave up his spirit.

St. John 19:30

WHEN JESUS DIED something had been achieved but in no sense was the purpose of his life finished. St. John and the early Church understood the words "it is finished" to refer to this achievement, the completion of a task. What Jesus achieved was a mind and heart completely open to God and life, daily offered to be the bearer of God's love in the world. He has become for us the outward and visible sign of what God's love is like.

Until its last moment, his last breath, there always hovered over his life the possibility of failure, of some extreme stress under which that concern for oneself that is the depressing flaw in all our efforts at loving would claim him too.

But he came through and, as he gave up his spirit, completed the task we believe to have been necessary for man's liberation from fear and from everything else that stifles love. To the Church thinking back on it all, and realizing how achievement and failure hung in the balance with increasing tension as the three hours wore on, it seemed that nothing in his life became him like the leaving it. It is no wonder that the term "the cross" figures so much in early Christian reflexion on the meaning of Jesus.

For us "the cross" is one of the great Christian code-words. We use it as a summary image to bring to our minds the thought of God's love declaring itself through the whole life, death and resurrection of Jesus.

What Jesus achieved does not stand on its own, exerting an influence on human affairs automatically, as though we receive some benefit simply by believing that he did what the Church says he did for us. There is nothing automatic in love. It is a living world of giving and taking, of gesture and response. Without the eager and affectionate response of men and women in the flowing years since his distant day, the life of Jesus would be no more than a broken column supporting nothing in the desert of time.

What he did has to be completed, by people hearing what is being said through it, letting it affect them and give form and hope to their lives. In this way their lives are dignified by becoming part of it; and he himself, with all he cared about and loved, goes on living in them.

This completion of his life, through people identifying themselves with him and themselves becoming offered to God and open to life, must go on until the end of the world.

The Church is the means by which people can enter into Jesus' self-offering and share it. It is the only place where what he did is believed in and talked about and continually discussed so that its infinite meaning may be explored. Its central and representative prayer is an endlessly repeated sacrament, the Eucharist, which gives us once more (it is never too late) the chance of coming back to him, regaining our spiritual bearings, and resuming our place, however unworthy, in that human response that fulfills all his loving.

The purpose of his earthly life was achieved the moment he died with his integrity intact. The thing he lived and died for was certainly not finished. There is no sign of its being finished even now, though there is Christian faith that it will be. What matters is that it should persist, with others living and dying for it day after day, that his kind of loving should continue to flow, a stream of meaning and inspiration to refresh and feed the spiritual life of the world.

St. John believed that this was all part of the intention of Jesus. He would have us read the concern of Jesus to bring together Mary and John before he died (the Mother and the Disciple) as representing his belief that there must be a body, a community, to be entrusted with his truth and to be the place of his sacramental presence. Indeed it may be that in this image of Jesus bowing his head and handing over the spirit St. John has let two meanings fuse in his meditative imagination, so that the end of the Jesus of history is the beginning of the Christ of faith as with solemn confidence and love he looks down and hands on to the Mother and the Disciple that for which and by which he had lived.[1]

In most lives spiritual achievement is closely related to the
unfinished, on-going character of life and to the whole of which
any life is a part. Jesus stayed with his assignment of life as
willingly as he could, trying to do with it something he believed
in as long as he had the power to do anything at all with it; and
then it was taken into what must have been to him an almost
unimaginable future.

Often in critical situations the most you can get around to
praying is the request for grace to stay with the thing life has
become. Perplexities and lonelinesses last for as long as they
can, none of them is eternal, and then they modify to become
the next situation. Our staying with them, trying to dignify
them with a bit of meaning is certain to put movement into
them. Simply to stare at them, longing for them to be over,
seems to make them stationary. In any experience of deprivation, if a person can accept and go through the pain of loss,
connecting it with what he already knows and believes about
life, the situation changes, begins to require from him new
responses which somehow seem to be available. If he does not
stay with it, shrinks from all its longing and temptation, clings
to his view of it as unbearable, he cannot manage the next
situation either. He goes into it as a person burdened with unfinished business, a man who has not grieved properly (worked
through his experience) and at the right time (when life was
truly grievous). He is that much shorter of experience and flexibility now. So, in Ibsen's play, Peer Gynt's attempt to take care
of himself results in his increasing impoverishment because so
much of what should and could have been his life he has simply
failed to live. For example, the weeping he could and should
have done comes to rebuke him in the sound of the drops of
dew falling from the trees:

> We are tears
> that were never shed;
> we might have melted
> the ice-spears that wounded you.

Now the barb festers
in your rough breast,
but the wound has closed over—
our power is gone.[2]

It is not that if we stay with our losses and frustrations and work through them we shall "get over" them more quickly. "Getting over" calamity is not at all a good idea. It is to empty intense and formidable experience of meaning and reduce it to the status of an interruption. What matters is to be alive. People run out of vitality either because their experience has been insufficient to provoke their generous response or has frightened it out of them, or because somebody or something in which they had invested all life's importance and beauty has been torn from them. Still, most people would agree that it is far better to know what pain is and how much it hurts than not to know. To suffer means always to lose something precious and be faced with the work of negotiating that loss. But not to suffer must surely amount to an incalculable loss. Jesus is said to have come in order to help people come fully alive. On this view, spiritual achievement is not the ability to get over things, or get by, but an openness to them so that they go through you with all their truth and test; it is the ability to hear what they are trying to tell you about life and so to be more alive.

It is implied that experience is worth having, even sorrows and humiliations, though no one would ever choose these. In one of his poems Rilke deplores the way we waste them. There is much to be said for the view that they have more to give us than joy though they could never give it in a life that was devoid of joy. The work of making sense of trouble builds the experience into oneself productively. It does not merely recede into the past, leaving only a fading memory of pain. To work through the initial fear and resentment and depression until one can take some hold of the situation, connect what has happened with one's general understanding of the way life goes, and begin to modify wishes and assumptions that now require some alteration—all this hard work makes the experience more part of

oneself than ever, and it is often rewarded by intimations of a
wholeness about life in which loss changes its character and
begins to look curiously like gain.

C. S. Lewis describes his own experience of this when his
wife had died and he was involved in the work of suffering it,
how one morning

> for various reasons, not in themselves at all mysterious, my
> heart was lighter than it had been for many weeks. . . . And
> suddenly at the very moment when, so far, I mourned H least,
> I remembered her best. Indeed it was something (almost) better
> than memory; an instantaneous, unanswerable impression. To
> say it was like a metting would go too far. Yet there was that in
> it which tempts one to use those words. It was as if the lifting
> of the sorrow removed a barrier.
>
> Why has no one told me these things? How easily I might
> have misjudged another man in the same situation? I might have
> said, "He's got over it. He's forgotten his wife," when the truth
> was, "He remembers her better *because* he has partly got over
> it." . . .
>
> For, as I have discovered, passionate grief does not link us
> with the dead but cuts us off from them. This becomes clearer
> and clearer. It is just at those moments when I feel least sor-
> row—getting into my morning bath is usually one of them—
> that H rushes upon my mind in her full reality, her otherness.
> Not, as in my worst moments, all foreshortened and patheti-
> cized and solemnized by my miseries, but as she is in her own
> right. This is good and tonic.[3]

If the achievement at which we are aiming is the spiritual
thing the New Testament continually offers us as the best in
life, we have clearly dispensed with achievement as usually
understood, as influence exerted, income increased, prestige
gained. We shall often have to look within to see whether we
have in fact discarded these delightful things. Christians are
often ludicrously and unbelievably high-souled about them. It
is wise to acknowledge their seduction, how they cling, return
when apparently dislodged, reappear with hallucinatory re-
spectability. But if the achievement we are hoping for is in fact

progress in responsiveness to life both outside and within ourselves, it needs to be understood that we are not going to be able to watch this, or measure it, or make it happen. It is not something that we produce at all. It is done by God, by love, and always when we ourselves are not looking.

In any case, any self we may consciously wish to achieve, even for the most laudable reasons, may well be anxiety-based, the outcome of some desire to be liked or to excel or to keep calm that has been nagging us for years. The saints frequently found that their great need was not for virtues to replace their sins; it was to let go their desire to do this and that for God because such desire was so often imposed on them by concealed personal vanities and compensatory strivings which never gave the tremendous love within them, the presence of God, a chance.

We can neither watch our progress nor achieve spiritual success but we can set about observing the conditions which leave the love which is God in us free to grow and express itself maturely and without fear. One of these conditions is the glad acceptance of the world's real presence.

One of the early and most necessary shocks a child has to undergo is the discovery that there is often a considerable difference between the world and one's thoughts about the world. A child slowly puts together the bits of truth out of which this crucial knowledge is made; that a feeling of sadness does not mean that the whole world is dark; that indeed in many experiences feelings and thoughts need to be looked at before you can know whether or not the situation is actually so; that changing but absorbing states of mind are highly personal and provisional affairs so that quite often reality does not square with one's own ideas and wishes but is much bigger and more powerful than them and tends to assert itself.

We have truly and marvelously begun to grow when we begin to acquire the skill of detaching ourselves from our experiences and make our first dispassionate check-ups on things and our thoughts about them. We never seem to acquire as much of this

skill as we need. It often seems to forsake us treacherously
when our emotions are engaged. So that spiritual growth certainly involves understanding the extraordinary power and
changeable character of our feelings, that they can be friends,
inspirers, deceivers, dominators, can lift us from our lamenta-
ble shallowness, can plunge us into hell. To be able to live with
them increasingly as friends and allies is a fine part of achieving
aliveness and openness. A person can be considered truly alive
for whom life has not been made rigid by one, over-protective
life-style but has remained flexible, who can see and seize al-
ternatives, who is able to postpone or re-route the gratification
of wanting and the expression of feeling when they conflict
with the desire of the deepest self.

That self is often buried and forgotten as we drift between
distractions but because it is the spirit in us it survives the trashy
years; and at any time it may be the means of our hearing a
voice that wakens us to all that matters, or of our experiencing
moments of truth and communion that make us ask ourselves
why so much of our life should be so trivial. Alive people are
open to their inwardness, they have come to know it gladly as
available energy to be used and genuine need to be met. And
we know that if it is ever given us to belong to that creditable
lot who have fought and seen it through to the end it will be
because this deep self has had its chance to enrich our being
and indicate the goals of our life.

The novelist Phyllis Bottome, in her autobiography, commented on her education and the good she had received from it
but acknowledged regretfully that the main task of life had not
even been presented to her: "I was unable to disassociate my
thoughts from my wishes, and therefore had no moral freedom." In later life she came to realize how much she wanted
freedom, and how important courage is to anyone who wants
it, because something in us resents the work involved in pre-
serving our freedom and will do much to escape it. "A man
cannot be free who prefers his short desires to his long ones.
He cannot be free if his dislikes are greater than his likes."[4]

Above all, he has no chance of remaining free if he cannot resist his world's tendency under stress and disappointment to contract to his current throb of personal feeling, if he is unable to insist that the whole of his experience of life shall have its say to the morose fraction that is hurting him just now.

Some practice in attention, even to the extent of deliberate exercises in observing, examining, feeling, must be part of praying if the world is to become a real presence to us. It may be that it is from this need that is to be traced the increasing use today of prayer in a simple but agreeable setting with no more visual aid than a candle-flame or a flower or some unrepresentative shape of wood or stone.

It is ridiculous to compare generations. We have no tools of measurement for such a delicate and cloudy exercise. But we think we know our own day. We have some sense of its spiritual nature though obviously we could be unduly confident in our perception of such an intricate matter. It does not seem to be a happy time. So much disappoints so many. So few find so little that strikes them as deserving celebration, perhaps because they have never been taught to look long and quietly enough at things and people and are in such a hurry to get through life that they are aware of it only as an undifferentiated flux that bears us along to tonight and then through a dark pause for recovery into tomorrow. There are not enough words of praise.

So much has been said and written in Christian circles about the superiority of the unseen to the seen that in order to avoid insulting the creator we need to hear the other argument. The other argument is that we should look very closely at the things that are seen precisely because they are temporal, because the daffodils indeed so soon fade, yet before they crumple under the sun they convey the world to us and ourselves to ourselves. The things that are eternal can presumably wait a bit until we have watched this and been duly shaken by it.

Dr. Martin Israel has suggested a form in which this exercise in attention might be practiced:

> With regard to the world around one, there should be a conscious willed period of attentiveness each day. It is the will that

has to be used to raise the consciousness from the depths of the self to the world outside. It is important to notice positively the objects in one's environment, the things in the familiar street, the flowers and trees in the garden and park, and above all the people one passes to and from one's work. Each is complete in itself, but it needs our recognition, just as we need the recognition of others to be fully human. If we do not trouble to recognize others because of inner preoccupation, no one will trouble to recognize us. It is important not only to recognize and acknowledge the uniqueness of each object and each person but also to flow out to them in silent gratitude for being what they are. All life in awareness is a blessing, and we show this by blessing those around us. This does not require a formula or an articulated statement; it is essentially an inner attitude.[5]

Aliveness and openness concern the world within as well as the world of things and people outside oneself. To grow in faith and hope and love, which is the only kind of maturity in which a believer can be seriously interested, will mean a gradual reaching better terms with one's continually active and frequently disappointing self. If it turns out that this spiritual achievement seems as much one of understanding and acceptance as of successful change there is no reason for surprise. To penetrate deeply into the characteristically Christian understanding of achievement must make continually clearer the importance that confession and forgiveness have in it. Jesus had alarming views of success as we normally understand the word, and unusually hopeful things to say about failure.

The hopefulness he saw in failure is worth all the attention needed to discern it. Its way of breaking down self-assurance and complacency puts it at once on the creative side of life, because no one ever improves who thinks he has arrived, and if he has in fact arrived the odds are that his journey was not necessary. There is no better way of learning compassion and forgiveness than through failure truly accepted. To be wrestling with something we may not be able to defeat will draw out all we have that is available at this stage; and if at day-break it is our limitations and not our power that we have limpingly to acknowledge, that in itself may well be a marvelous form of seeing God face to face and finding one's life preserved.

Certainly the more we understand that seeing ourselves in spirit and in truth is seeing God face to face and that this is how life is served and preserved the less we shall need to withdraw from life because this or that area of it makes us afraid or resentful.

This outcome is not to be recommended because fear and resentment are always evil. On the contrary, they are God-given providers of energy for experiences where fear is appropriate or some unjust situation needs to be resisted and changed. Similarly, a mature love is an honest, outgoing love for the truly loveable, not a dependence on someone who is covertly being used to supply some missed affection of a vanished time like childhood. Spiritual growth is this increasing ability to match feelings and situations, to be emotionally honest, and at the same time to acknowledge to the full the legitimacy and power and risk to them of other people's feelings. Immaturity will then be assumed when a person behaves in a way unsuited to the current situation but quite appropriate to some earlier stage in his development. In the life of faith, people's prayers and their idea of God (the two are so close as to be almost two sides of one coin) are frequently out of date in this way—they do not seem to belong to anything they are doing or suffering now.

Of course, such people may easily have been extremely unfortunate in their teachers. There are other ways, too, in which aliveness and sensitiveness to existence indicate growth but depend too much on luck, education and other creative influences in one's life. Ideally, the spiritual life should mean that more of this world should arouse our feelings and so extend and diversify our emotional experience. Good fortune will inevitably come into that, though the will to be interested must always be there, ready to take the chances that come.

In the second half of life there is a natural movement of the imagination towards being rather than doing, away from prestige-motivated acquisition and accomplishment, and tentatively towards life's meaning, whether or not conscious religion has been important in the preceding years. There is usually a growth of concern about what things need more tenderness than they are getting, how much one's marriage needs re-shaping, how you are to bear the world's beauty when you have reached that point in the journey when you have a strong suspicion that the end of your life is following you.

All this is some of the full life we believe Jesus wanted people to have and tried to bring to their notice. It is not the monopoly of Christians. There have been other explorers of the spiritual through whom the holy spirit of God has articulated to enrich and heal life in a world as complicated as it is fascinating. We think of the true achievement in spiritual terms because the word "spiritual" refers to life as it is registered in the depths of the self, by the self as it responds to the world in its most reverent and wholehearted moments, and because the awarenesses of a life so deeply and wholeheartedly lived have had an unmistakable beckoning role in human life throughout the centuries. There is a tendency to underestimate people's ability to understand and find excitement in such inwardness, where the roots of any genuine love and joy and peace they are going to have must necessarily lie. Some time ago, newspapers carried a dramatic and entertaining account of an intrepid English actress who had followed a strange inner summons to make a success of bull-fighting in Spain. This she had considerably achieved but to her surprise without the satisfaction she had expected. Her summary comment was, "There are greater forms of bravery. Simply getting from day to day is braver." Not everyone would agree that that particular truth was correctly marked at the price she curiously had to pay for it; but all spiritual meanings can be seen as forms of that light of our ignorance and companion of our journey which we have called Christ.

Our response to truth is an unpredictable affair, sometimes eager, often disturbingly inadequate. It seems to depend on how much of ourselves is available for giving. There is truth that merely brightens and intrigues the mind for a while, and truth which we are able to take deeply into ourselves to help us make a more constructive response to our challenges and anxieties. To be alive and open must involve being able to use insights in this way, so that we modify the way we are living, because if we are unable to adjust to the continual changes of our world we are bound to stagnate. The mature person is one who has grown simply through having been able to change.

Our unwillingness to change is a form of our reluctance to think and pray in spirit and in truth. When we confront it we can at any rate be sure that there is nothing false about this, we are dealing with reality, with God and ourselves.

If we were willing to change we would not so often try to avoid truth or keep it at a distance. Yet it is part of the grace of things that the willingness hides somewhere within us, whatever our evasions and subterfuges, and bides its time.

The friends of Jesus must have found living with him a similar perplexity. For them he was a way of seeing their world for the first time. The fact that a man like him existed at all made life a new thing altogether; that they knew he wanted them made it infinitely important. And his way of living in the present, without the drag of yesterday, without dread of what might be coming, yet with beliefs, habits, hopes that suggested a man whose most trivial action was a response to an inner ordering of his whole life—all this produced a peculiar silence in them and the sense that they were being led towards events and experiences for which they had no attitudes prepared. Yet go with him, in love, they must. It was their desire. They frequently quarreled among themselves and with him, often wondered how much longer they could put up with the endless work of understanding him and what he so desperately seemed to want them to understand. They would think of shaking free; and then would come the heavy tug of a deeper truth, that they absolutely belonged to him, a truth made joyful by his extraordinary power of convincing them that what they could yet be was all in the summons and promise of the love that moves the sun and the other stars.

The life of Christian faith has been a continual recapitulation of that original experience. It is a matter of working into our lives the meanings and aspirations that come with the gift of faith, being ready to question our defenses and aggressions now that we have some conviction of God's care, learning how to accept limits and what limits to accept, trying out what silence can do for a man of today who wants God, attempting to simplify life—and a hundred other things, to say nothing of the discoveries, the connections and significances that bring the reality of God, with a shock of surprise and sometimes intense irritation, into pleasures and pains with which he had little to do previously. And slowly the important changes begin.

For example, the spirit works in us a more honest and also less merciless attitude to ourselves; and consequently our attitude to others is freed from the burden of our projections and can become sympathetic. The sheer interest of a life of purpose and hope, as contrasted with meaningless drifting, lifts from us the need to clutch at other people with demands for love that no one can satisfy; and consequently we are less disappointed in people and can like them more. In such piecemeal and gradual ways a conversion is worked at, and spiritual growth proceeds.

It is, however, profoundly complicated and retarded by a number of factors which together add up to that unwillingness to change and to let changes come which is a chronic problem with most of us.

The first of these is simply that the work is hard. It is not always easy to take the words of Jesus and apply them to oneself. He said some dreadful things; some of them terrified his first friends as much as they do us. Most people, before they begin the life of faith, have already been marking themselves a lot lower than beta in their private reflections and under the pain of this have seriously reduced their capacity for rational self-scrutiny. They may become convinced that they cannot take criticism from any source whatever and can only react to it with aggression or despair in one form or another. They may have stopped having spiritual wants for this reason. Yet the only result must be not to know oneself at all; people cannot know what they want if they do not allow themselves to have wants.

While some spiritual growth is almost automatic, because it is the result of deeper change, much progress seems clearly a work of co-operation with God on some area of life that has come into question. Much mishandling of life is the result of patterns of behavior adopted in the past to allay anxiety. They may no longer be needed and indeed may be an infernal nuisance, but to question them and their usefulness raises the old fears again. It requires more than persuasion to convince people that such dreads are only ghosts now.

In working through bereavement, the clear need for fresh sources of supply, or the greater use of those to hand, in the recovery of a sense of life's continued joy is quite difficult to see and harder still to act on simply because seeing it underlines the fact that the one great joy has in fact gone and the grieving lover may not be ready yet for such complete acceptance.

The ways in which we may resist change in our chosen mode of living life are innumerable. They vary greatly in seriousness and so in the degree to which they block our spiritual growth. But the attitude or reaction that needs to be altered, because it is in some way restricting our life or preventing the growth of new powers and deeper satisfactions, has usually at its root the fact that it was adopted (however misguidedly) as a means of coping with some fear or humiliation or rejection.

The work is certainly hard. But the life of faith is not all hard work. The friends of Jesus found that they could not leave him even when they felt they had had enough of him. There was that in him which just held them or drew them back. It was good to be still and know that he was there. It was good to sit at his feet and hear his word. The spiritual life is fed by contemplation as well as meditation and cannot dispense with either.

Every small progress in the life of love, every fresh understanding achieved, makes individuals less afraid of themselves and reduces their sense that life is against them. They begin to feel less alone and more hopeful. The spiritual life, as Christians understand it, is a presence and a hope within the believer. It is the work of the spirit of God in the depths of the self. Believers can trust the work of that spirit to go on of itself as long as they do their part.

Their part is to give time to developing their faith. As they cultivate the life of faith, the trusts and reverences and confidences that formed the mind of Jesus begin to grow in them to invigorate and redirect their life. But it is always from within outward, not a set of checks and controls they impose on their behavior in yet one more attempt to bring it into line but a new inner life, begun as soon as we turn to God, at a depth at first beyond our perception but where all genuine love that brightens human life has its root.

It is the presence within of that spirit, both a drive and need for life, for fulfillment, that makes self-scrutinies productive and the pain of maturing acceptable. It can give us willingness to relinquish strategies and satisfactions that constituted our amateurish and not very trustworthy safety. It encourages us to try new ways of managing our emotional life even though at first they may not seem to work so well.

The prayer that rightly accompanies this work of spiritual growth is the natural relaxation that is complementary to work. It is the prayer by which we detach ourselves from our experiences and problems, a simple prayer of faith and attention to God, a waiting on him as one who is at work deep within and will finish that good thing he has begun. The prayer is not meditative, that is to say, a matter of thinking through such religious expectation, but the simple, almost wordless, expression of desire.

It is this kind of prayer that God uses to build in us a foundation of hope. There is no spiritual progress at all without hope. Whenever we have to make changes in our lives, or accept those that have occurred, there is no doubt that we shall resist unless we can see that though the change involves loss it is under God some kind of gain or growth of deepened knowledge of what love is. This infinitely creative expectation about the essential grace of things is God's gift of hope. It does not need specification. People who feel that their lives are mysteriously unfolding because of some deep experience, are in some interesting way on the move, often say that it is not a matter of achieving some end they have set themselves or realizing some purpose but a basically happy looking and waiting for something to be revealed.

The anonymous author of *The Cloud of Unknowing* is continually encouraging his readers to develop this kind of waiting on God:

> . . . lift your heart to God with humble love. And really mean God himself who created you, and bought you, and graciously called you to this state of life. And think no other thought of him. It all depends on your desire. A naked intention directed to God, and himself alone, is wholly sufficient.
>
> If you want this intention summed up in a word, to retain it more easily, take a short word, preferably of one syllable, to do so . . . A word like "God" or "Love." Choose which you like, or perhaps some other, so long as it is of one syllable. And fix this word fast to your heart, so that it is always there come what may . . . if ever you are tempted to think what it is that you are seeking, this one word will be sufficient answer.[6]

7

GIVING

Then Jesus, crying with a loud voice, said, "Father, into thy hands I commit my spirit!" And having said this he breathed his last.

St. Luke 23:46

THE WORDS "Into thy hands I commit my spirit" come from the marvelously sustaining tradition of prayer that had been the breath of life to Jesus.[1] The word "Father," and the intimacy and affection with which Jesus used it in his own language when he addressed God,[2] was an entirely new sound and meaning in human experience. It conveys the authentic voice of Jesus and the aura of his being so clearly and at such depth that anyone wanting to understand him could very well begin with Jesus' use of this word for God.

Christianity is a difficult religion, difficult to understand. But it is not only quite understandable but also a great help to us that the basic Christian prayer should be known as the "Our Father." Its conventional title brings to mind immediately this central word in Jesus' religious talk; and the prayer itself is an infinitely important unfolding of the way in which Jesus thought God could be meaningfully addressed, what he always wanted to say in God's presence, and the things for which he thought it is worthwhile approaching God.

The prayer begins by suggesting that it is right to accept things, as they are, as the outcome and expression of the providential care of God seen in Jesus' characteristic way as a loving Father. This is the initial Christian stance. All the questions and complaints that naturally arise in the human mind arise for the Christian within this initial attitude to experience. Indeed it is this posture before life that provokes the complaints and questions. If you begin by believing that God is a monster who requires human sacrifice, or that he is incapable of what humans wistfully regard as care, or is simply a word that now refers to nothing that is real though it once carried some significant part of man's aspiration, you will not be shocked by certain outrageous and unjust features of human life that do shock people who believe that he is a loving father. But the view of Jesus is that first, before all the questioning and complaining, we take the view that all is from the hands of a loving father. Christians will, and are indeed invited to, question what God does and allows, but prior to all that they believe that God's name is to be hallowed, that is to say, God himself, the providential order, the way things unfortunately happen to me, is right, is holy, is the revelation of an infinite love.

The world certainly does not look as if it is that kind of thing. Christianity exists to say that it is, and to commend the idea as one which fits human experience better than any other. One would not argue at length for it, mainly because the Christian church has always warned people about faith, saying that you have as much chance of finding God at the end of an argument as you have of finding a pot of gold at the end of a rainbow. Faith is a gift to the mind, not a discovery by the mind. That has always been the Christian view. But faith naturally seeks understanding, wishes to relate itself to the facts. There is no fact that must of necessity be understood in a way that is inconsistent with God's fatherly presence.

Jesus spoke carefully about that fatherly presence. He was an honest man and would not give you anything false or exaggerated. Where he stood you could stand too. We have to listen to what he said; we have to hear what he did not say.

For example, he did not say that death is the wages of sin. He did not say that God would save his friends from the violence of life; indeed he warned them to be prepared for it.

However, he did say that not a sparrow falls to the ground without God the Father. What could one ask of such a God? One would ask for the faith that carried Jesus through, the certainty that when you fall you are not alone.

Mr. D. Z. Phillips has imagined someone praying in a storm:

"O God, don't let the lightning hit my house." Sometimes this almost seems to mean, "Let the lightning hit someone else's house!" What is one to say about that kind of prayer? One can say that one does not like it, but that is neither here nor there. The prayer reveals the attitude of the person concerned to the way things go. It reveals little devotion, since, if the house were hit, one could imagine the event resulting in loss of faith.[3]

If faith were lost for such a reason we would think that the believer had never understood Jesus.

The philosopher Wittgenstein has said: "Love is not a feeling. Love is put to the test, pain not. One does not say: 'That was not true pain, or it would not have gone off so quickly.'"[4] Similarly, faith is not a feeling. Unlike a feeling, faith is put to the test. Faith that passes away because of something unpleasant happening to you could not be true faith as Christians understand faith. Jesus trusted in God as one who holds to us through good and ill, waiting to give and be given to in every situation, so that anywhere may become the place where faith and love light the world. The Father was for him the inseparable presence, in life, in death, in what has happened now, in what will happen tomorrow.

We begin to understand why the Lord's prayer was not a commonplace in the early Church. Being the heart of Jesus' faith, when it was in fact said it was said with deep reverence and awe that we have such a God and that life makes so much intense meaning when continually referred to him. The early Christian view was that the whole matter of faith is yours if you can say it.[5]

"Are not two sparrows sold for a farthing? And not one of them falls to the ground without your Father"; "Father, into thy hands I commit my spirit." This man sees all natural events as within the purpose and caring of God. For Jesus, death itself is included in the divine fatherliness and like any other experience is in principle an occasion for giving to God until we have to give up even the power of giving. He said little about it. Certainly he did not see death as posing a problem for the mind and putting a strain on faith. The problem was elsewhere, in man's failure to love. To his mind, not to love was not to live. He longed to rescue people from that death, so much so that the other death was comparatively insignificant.

It is not insignificant to people of today. Perhaps there is not so much fear of death itself as there used to be. The twentieth-century dread is attached to the approach to death, particularly to the possibility of protracted enfeeblement, because there has been a change in the quality of family love and people are afraid of the test which their helplessness may mean for it. As the great unavoidable unknown, death must always alarm, but old age is a wider and bleaker landscape than formerly; its possibilities in loss of dignity, loneliness, reversal to dependence on others' shifting interest and tolerance bring an insecurity into our second childhood that our first never had.

Life and death mirror one another strangely. One's attitude to either seems to reflect one's feeling about the other. To those for whom the old assurances about the life beyond have gone, death all the more calls into question this life's meaning. If you have no equipment, in the form of a vocabulary and a set of values, for entertaining such a large question, anything that brings it to mind will also bring the flutter and tremble of anxiety. You will be driven to avoid the subject. The often noted silence about death in our culture is as much a product of this intellectual helplessness and dismay as it is of fear. The cliché about death being the taboo subject for our generation that sex was for the Victorian world has the characteristic insensitiveness of superficial smartness. It is part of the deep sadness of our time that if people exclude death from their thoughts, for whatever reason, it is the more likely to overwhelm them when it comes too near.

There is, however, a positive value in the extension of modern anxiety from the experience of dying to the tract of old age preceding it. Death is not most usefully considered by itself. It belongs with other more accessible matters. Jesus was concerned with this life and the possibility of its being lived as loving and giving, at any time, whatever one's age. It is just a fact that when life is so lived death does not loom sinisterly, does not unduly attract attention, and is indeed most successfully, because indirectly, prepared for.

Our ability to love and give is blocked most by our fears and antipathies. Our fears and antipathies are the deposit of our vision of the world as in some sense hostile or threatening our security. Beneath every failure to love there is some conviction

that it is not safe to give oneself affectionately and spontaneously to life. No one is free from some degree of this fear. It
is commonly thought to have deep roots that reach into the
obscurities of our earliest experiences. In order to silence it we
are driven to various policies of attack, withdrawal and com-
pliance (sometimes in illogical and conflicting mixture). These
become established attitudes with a momentum of their own so
that they may in fact be no longer relevant to the situation before us, though once they were. To this perennial human perplexity Jesus brought faith in the unchanging fatherly presence
of God, in the rightness of trusting life to be working for you
all the time, in the unnecessariness of fear. As this faith is
steadily worked into daily experience, our hidden dreads and
angers begin to dissolve and our power to love and give is released. People who love life and love giving to it and receiving
from it do not find themselves particularly perturbed about death.

We cannot be working at this all the time; but certain areas
of our life reveal our fears and antipathies with some regularity.
We might well consider them spiritually under-developed re-
gions calling for help. One is the experience of change, our
shakiness in the presence of any situation which involves giving
up one arrangement and re-organizing our life in a new pattern.
Various apprehensions may unnerve us which are really all the
same fear—that we shall not be able to manage without this or
that relationship, environment, idea on whose support we have
come to depend. The prop that makes life steady for us could
be entirely mental, like the sense of significance gained from
our daily work or some fantasy of our ability of knowledge or
rectitude that operates so obscurely in our relationships and
judgements we rarely see it though others may. Whatever it is,
when it is challenged by the prospect of change or by contra-
dictory experience we register alarm and look round for some
form of protection. This defensiveness is mostly no help to us
at all. The odds are that we ought to be ready to change. Unless
we change we cannot grow.

Some people are naturally defenseless, and that is why they radiate so much liveliness. They can give the self which others labor to protect. The rest of us, especially when we have passed the middle years and it is time to confront oneself and estimate life from a second position, need to question the fears that fence us in. Christian spirituality makes much room for cultivating the sense of the grace inherent in life's change and growth and for learning to expect change and growth in ourselves. It is work that belongs particularly to the second half of life; the fact is emphasized in eastern religion and ought to be more openly acknowledged in Christian teaching, especially as most of those who are exposed to Christian counsel are at this stage of the journey. It is sometimes argued that this spiritual work of shifting the emphasis of one's life from doing to being, from manipulating existence in the interests of purpose to acquiring openness to it and to new ranges of it, is so important as to deserve a special act of commitment from the Christian, a second calling or confirmation, with appropriate liturgical expression.

At one time the work of this stage of life was mistakenly described as preparation for death. The Christian life is not a preparation for anything; it is a learning how to live here and now in freedom from fear and self-concern, in open faith and hope and love. Something like this kind of life, we believe, is in God's purpose for us after death, but we do not learn it for that reason but for its absolute validity. The life of the spirit in the Christian view is one thing this side and the other side of the grave. Thornton Wilder's words can be understood in a deeply Christian sense: "There is a land of the living and a land of the dead, and the bridge is love, the only survival, the only meaning."[6]

To be open to experience and ready for whatever awarenesses may come is the route to a full life whether one has or has not religious faith in the formal sense. To be truly open to life and able to receive from it and give to it enthusiastically must involve accepting the fact that death is a certainty one day

and a possibility any day for me and for those I love. Martin
Heidegger has pointed out that you could not take seriously
anyone's claim to be free who had not achieved this personal
appropriation of mortality; that is to say, ideally it is part of
maturity (because the young mind is not open to this) to be free
to die now. It is part of the fascinating statement which Christianity carries that life cannot be loved and lived to the uttermost
unless at the same time not far below the surface of the mind
is the readiness for this day to be one's last.

If we were genuinely free of our own death we could use the
thought of it. It would not be so sharpened by fear that it would
hurt. We would value the positive light it throws back on life,
the way it exposes worthwhileness and triviality. There are pur-
suits and ways of living which look as good as new in the
thought of death. If it came soon or late, and you had chance
to reflect, you would be glad of those human times, you would
not wish to alter things, though of course desiring more of
these. There are others it slowly undermines or shows up with
shocking ridicule. Every life has these mistakes, failures in
discernment, disgraces. The thought which makes it clear to us
that life does not deserve to be so manhandled has done us a
service. Goodness, dignity, responsibility breathe through it.

The only form in which death comes into view for many
people is the death of others. Many people may have little anxiety about their own death yet not much ability to use the thought
of it but still be overwhelmed by its apparent power to destroy
relationships. To those who have no faith in a life beyond, the
destruction of their loves is an assignment of suffering just as
grueling as it is for Christians and others who do believe. They
suffer in a different mental world, with different intellectual
supports, different ceremonials of memory and gratitude. But
everyone has to learn how to suffer in heart and mind and soul,
that is to say, thoroughly and intelligently, so that life is not
filled with bitterness but to some extent purified and enlight-
ened for our continuance with it till the evening falls. All of us
have to try to save our beloved dead from the silence to which

convention increasingly seems to consign them.

The churches are reluctant to use the fullness of the faith for which they exist, and not surprisingly, because they do not form a separate world but breathe the one atmosphere of intellectual hesitation that inflates this generation's lungs. There is however no need for a Christian believer to apologize for thinking that God's purpose for our dead is that they shall still work with us in Christ. It is not sufficient that the dead have just one day every year and that they be given the year's last flowers. It is certainly not true that because there is not enough love to go round it is inevitably the dead who must go without. Love is not some stock that can be exhausted. The more loving is done the more power love has in the world. It can draw a bit of strength even from the self-communing world of love for an animal that is the comfort of thousands of solitaries in the depths of our great cities, because whatever is genuine in that love, whatever is real gift to another, is significant beyond the lonely room that is its setting. The infinitely hopeful and happy faith in the communion of saints is not an annual commemoration for Christians but the inner reality of every Eucharist. God meant this holy communion to be, as part of the mystery of Christ, an endlessly repeated signal to grief, that we are still together, branches of the one vine. The vital sap of his love runs through the whole. So it is not too late to do them good, to give them our love and to want theirs, to understand those we could not love and why we could not, and to come into that light in which our fears and accusations wither and our choked love is released.

New Testament writers make much of the faith that to see the world as God's presence is really to have everything for which you were created, so that the life after death cannot be anything which in principle you do not know though its form and quality will be infinitely richer than anything eye has seen or ear heard and its mystery is too great for the mind of man to grasp now. There is great play with the ideas of foretaste and anticipation, that in the new life of faith and hope and love into which our conversion is leading us we have already begun the life beyond. It is not now the absolutely unknown. In our approximations to Jesus' way of loving and trusting we have a glimpse of it, like the bright light of a next room shining under the door.

It is thought that the glimpse will come more frequently and grow in power. Christian spirituality today is better off with images of life and growth and change than with the vocabulary of dying, though that has been extensively used in the past and notably by Jesus himself. To be willing to grow and therefore to change is certainly the only way of experiencing the world as the presence of God. Important experience, beautiful or dreadful, which brings us a new knowledge of ourselves or a new understanding of life will indeed do this only if we respond to it sufficiently to absorb it and to want to learn from it; and this must mean allowing ourselves to be altered by it. This may be painful, but it is change and the surrender of some retarding security and the management of pain that are involved, not dying. To say "Father, into thy hands I commit my spirit" is to accept the risk of life.

Generations of Christians have said those words every day in Compline, the night prayers of the community. They could just as appropriately be said at any of the daily offices from dawn to dusk. They represent the giving of oneself to God as he comes in one's experiences. Every experience is an opportunity of giving oneself to him, by doing, enjoying, enduring whatever work or delight or pain the situation carries. God is the only reality worthy of any human being's surrender. We should not give ourselves to some other. It is the great sadness in suicide, according to the Christian view, that it is not possible to say to God "Into thy hands" while seeking one's death, because it is not possible to say "Into thy hands" to God out of fear or hatred of the life in which the presence of God is waiting to bless you. We have all been summoned from nonbeing into being for this purpose—to become a self who can in some sense offer what there is of him to God and life.

The spiritual life is about our growth and change, and our shrinking from this out of a mistaken vision of it as a danger instead of a fulfillment. Certainly to love someone deeply (even if the love ends) means to be quite changed by the experience. In a novel by Lawrence Durrell someone observes that when you pluck a flower the branch springs back into place but this is not true of the heart's affections. If you give yourself to another in trust and honesty there is change; memory carries a mark now, giver and receiver remain turned to one another, to which curious relatedness is to be traced the risk of hurt in love. The only way not to be changed is not to love; and that brings a more sinister risk:

> To love at all is to be vulnerable. Love anything, and your heart will certainly be wrung and possibly be broken. If you want to make sure of keeping it intact, you must give your heart to no-one, not even to an animal. Wrap it carefully around with hobbies and little luxuries; avoid all entanglements; lock it up safe in the casket or coffin of your selfishness. But in that casket—safe, dark, motionless, airless—it will change. It will not be broken; it will become unbreakable, impenetrable, irredeemable. The alternative to tragedy, or at least to the risk of tragedy, is damnation. The only place outside Heaven where you can be safe from all the dangers and perturbations of love is Hell.[7]

That comment on the way things go is by a Christian, but its truth is that sanity of the spirit that unites individuals of a dozen creeds and none. If people are able to grow in love, increasing the initial welcome they give to their experiences and to the work of making them in some way carriers of life, from whatever source they draw this spiritual vitality and knowledge, they do seem to become freer; and their freedom is freedom to love and give more sensitively and costlily.

This freedom inevitably alters the look of things. Particularly it alters the appearance of pain and death, makes them matter less, diminishes their fearsome character, and all because of the way in which loving and giving turn experience to the right side of life's account.

Christians' faith in eternal life is the product of a vast and varied experience of this freedom, and the hope it stimulates, drawn from the source of all their freedom and hope which is Christ. They are not making the irritating claim to know more about the future than others. They are presenting a way of seeing the present and negotiating its joy, its movement and anxiety.

They are often accused of wishful thinking. No doubt they do that kind of thing, since everyone wishes. And everyone has some wishes he knows about and some that hide in the inaccessible depths of his inwardness, from which they pour their sweetness or bitterness into his thoughts without discovery.

But it is a curious thing that we cannot imagine non-being. When we think about our death we assume the continuance of the thinker. Consequently the odds are that we are not truly investigating but making some subjective use of the idea. Well, it is possible to wish one's thought of death's finality not to be disturbed. It can give protection quite efficiently—an end to the burden of responsible selfhood, the one "place" where it is possible to hide from God and indeed from life. Christian believers are aware of this only because they catch themselves playing with the idea too, in times when what they think is their deeper insight fades.

No one *knows* the answer to this most ancient of all the questions. Some may prefer dogmatic denial to faith and hope, finding it helpful to close the issue. There are others who believe that not knowing is a stimulus to growing, and that it is good for us that God does not disclose himself on our terms.

However, when it is a matter of life and death there is a dissatisfaction and a feeling of impropriety about arguing. What matters is that everyone should stand where he can, in the world he sees when he really tries to see, and that what he denies and what he affirms should result in the increase of his own freedom and his readiness to help others to theirs.

"Into thy hands I commit my spirit." Originally part of a prayer of a Jew in trouble who never dreamed of the use one day to be made of his words, they represent a man's giving

himself to God. Their use in the Old Testament and with tremendous solemnity by Jesus, and in unspecifiable frequency
since, has given them spiritual authority. Always is the time for
this, this gift of oneself to what is present, to the bit of life here
and now, and to God clearly or dimly perceived in it by faith.
Whatever is true, honorable, just and lovely invites this gift
from us so persuasively that our reluctances are often quite
demolished. Whatever is frightening, lonely and painful is another matter. There the call to give oneself to the God who is
present puts faith to the test.

In one of his letters Baron von Hügel writes about the usefulness of seeing failure to love God as a fear or evasion of
some pain or loneliness or effort involved in doing his will.
Another way of looking at it is as an unwillingness to give up
some defensive pride or withdrawal that we have chosen to
protect us from the risk and effort of loving. He recommends
that whenever we face any kind of difficulty or pain in which
God's will is to be done, we should pray, at the moment itself,
without delay or evasion, as spontaneously as possible, that this
experience may deepen us and help to make us real, "really
humble, really loving, really ready to live or die with my soul
in thy hands." The all-important point is to do this "*at the time*
and *with the pain* well mixed up into the prayer."[8]

That would be genuine prayer, a prayer of faith. More often
than not God is not discerned, is groped for but not found, is
addressed in faith alone; but later, when we have come through
and we begin to interpret that good fact, he is found to have
been there in power. Every time anyone wholeheartedly accepts
what comes, endeavoring to do God's will in it and to make
some gesture of love and trust out of it, he is released from
some of his habitual fearing and resenting and made able to put
out more love and trust.

In bits and episodes the new life comes, occasionally dramatically, like a resurrection, but normally as a growth of love,
made possible by the reduction of fear and by willingness to
change. This pattern of growth is widely observable, showing

through life at many points. In the life of individuals, institutions, churches, nations, it is always relevant to see the present situation in terms of an arrangement for meeting a need or for protection against a threat, its one-time usefulness, its current restrictive power, and the need for change to a new adaptation to reality. The conviction grows that by such means God wills us to know that life is good and to have a growing appetite for it.

Life is not survival. To struggle for survival is to believe in yesterday, to have settled for some finality and to want it to stand even though it is no longer working. That is to have invited death in, whether the struggle concerns a personal longing that an individual dare not give up or a political or religious orthodoxy in whose terms alone some group finds the meaning of its existence.

Those who have been most ready for all God's perfect will, in its continual movement of changing call and blessing, have found their readiness met by a gift of faith that neither life nor death can separate us from an endless purpose of fulfillment. We have not sufficient words and ideas to explain what it means for a purpose to be endless, for God to have that purpose, for us to have that fulfillment. Death, time, space, our limited vocabulary and the limits of speech itself stand in the way. For centuries religious people have thrown words at what is hinted to us, in our mixed human experience, not doing well at outlining that of which they were certain, but often conveying the power of their certainty marvelously. That is probably as much as can be communicated to someone who is strangely a stranger to the glimpses of eternity, the beckonings of the transcendent, which in fact have thrilled innumerable people. The certainty of faith in God's endless purpose for us might be rendered by saying that the more we give ourselves into his hands in our successive encounters with joy and pain the more we are in the hands of life. St. Paul, thinking of the last of those temporal encounters, said that what is sown in the earth as a perishable thing is raised imperishable. It is a very powerful and justly famous way of putting it: "So is it with the resurrection of the dead. What is sown is perishable, what is raised is imperishable. It is sown in dishonor, it is raised in glory. It is sown in weakness, it is raised in power. It is sown a physical body, it is raised a spiritual body."⁹

NOTES

Chapter 1

1. T. S. Eliot, *Four Quartets: The Complete Poems and Plays* (Faber and Faber, 1969), p. 182.
2. St. Matthew 18:21-34.
3. *The Foolishness of God* (Darton, Longman and Todd, 1970), p. 386.

Chapter 2

1. Saul Bellow, *Herzog* (Weidenfeld and Nicolson, 1965), p. 317.
2. Jorge Luis Borges, *A Personal Anthology*, ed. Anthony Kerrigan, tr. Irving Feldman (Pan Books, 1972), p. 147.
3. Peter Berger, *A Rumour of Angels* (Pelican Books, 1971), p. 80.
4. Peter Berger, op. cit., p. 83.
5. Gabriel Marcel, *Homo Viator*, tr. Emma Craufurd (Gollancz, 1951), p. 46.
6. Gabriel Marcel, op. cit., p. 67.
7. T. S. Eliot, *Four Quartets: The Complete Poems and Plays* (Faber and Faber, 1969), p. 180.
8. E. Lampert, *The Apocalypse of History*, p. 66.

Chapter 3

1. Max Thurian, *Mary, Mother of the Lord, Figure of the Church*, tr. N. Cryer (Faith Press, 1963), pp. 162, 201 (n. 43); Raymond Brown, *The Gospel According to St. John* (Geoffrey Chapman, 1971), pp. 99, 107-9, 924-6.
2. *The Cloud of Unknowing*, tr. Clifton Wolters (Penguin Books, 1961), pp. 53, 60.
3. Antonia White, *The Hound and the Falcon* (Longman Group, 1965), (Collins Fontana Books, 1969), p. 211.
4. Timothy Ware, "The Communion of Saints," in *The Orthodox Ethos* (Holywell Press, Oxford, 1964), vol. 1, p. 142.

5. Baron Friedrich von Hügel, *Selected Letters,* ed. Bernard Holland (Dent, 1928), p. 230.
6. René Laurentin, in *Nouvelle Revue Théologique,* May 1967, pp. 502-3.
7. Hugh MacDiarmid, *Collected Poems,* Revised Edition (Macmillan Publishing Co. Inc., 1962).

Chapter 4
1. Charles Rycroft, *Anxiety and Neurosis* (Penguin Books, 1970), p. 107.
2. D. Z. Phillips, *The Concept of Prayer* (Routledge and Kegan Paul, 1965), p. 67.
3. Konrad Lorenz, *Civilized Man's Eight Deadly Sins,* tr. M. Latzke (Methuen, 1974), pp. 28, 76.
4. Colette, *Earthly Paradise,* ed. Robert Phelps (Secker and Warburg, 1974), p. 12.
5. T. S. Eliot, *Four Quartets: The Complete Poems and Plays* (Faber and Faber, 1969), p. 186.

Chapter 5
1. T. S. Eliot, "Little Gidding." The words are a quotation from *The Cloud of Unknowing,* chapter 2.
2. Thomas Traherne, *Centuries of Meditations* (Dobell, 1934), pp. 3-4.
3. Bertrand Russell, *Autobiography* (Unwin Books, 1975), p. 303.
4. Simone Weil, *Waiting for God* (Routledge and Kegan Paul, 1952), p. 149.
5. St. Luke 10:25-37.
6. C. S. Lewis, *The Screwtape Letters* (Collins Fontana, 1960), p. 76.
7. Joanna Field, *A Life of One's Own* (Penguin Books, 1955), p. 177.
8. La Rochefoucauld.

Chapter 6
1. R. E. Brown, *The Gospel according to St. John* (Geoffrey Chapman, 1972), pp. 910, 931. See also p. 55.
2. Henrik Ibsen, *Peer Gynt,* tr. Peter Watts (Penguin Books, 1972), p. 195.

3. C. S. Lewis, *A Grief Observed* (Faber and Faber, 1961), pp. 37, 44.
4. Phyllis Bottome, *Search for a Soul*, pp. 313, 317.
5. Martin Israel, M. B., *An Approach to Spirituality*, published by the Churches' Fellowship for Psychical and Spiritual Studies, 1971, p. 28. Excellent recommendations on this point can be found in the essay "On Praying" by Alan Ecclestone in *Spirituality for Today*, edited by Eric James.
6. *The Cloud of Unknowing*, tr. Clifton Wolters (Penguin Books, 1961), pp. 61, 62.

Chapter 7

1. Psalm 31:5.
2. "Abba"—"dear Father": cf. Jeremias, *The Prayers of Jesus* (SCM, London, 1967), pp. 95-98.
3. D. Z. Phillips, *The Concept of Prayer* (Routledge and Kegan Paul, 1965), p. 118.
4. L. Wittgenstein, *Zettel*, tr. G. E. M. Anscombe (Blackwell, 1967), para. 504.
5. J. Jeremias, *The Prayers of Jesus* (SCM Press, 1967), pp. 97, 98.
6. Thornton Wilder, *The Bridge of San Luis Rey*.
7. C. S. Lewis, *The Four Loves* (Collins Fontana, 1963), pp. 111-12.
8. Baron von Hügel, *Selected Letters*, ed. Bernard Holland (Dent, 1928), p. 232.
9. 1 Corinthians 15:42-44.

QUESTIONS
FOR GROUP DISCUSSION
AND PERSONAL REFLECTION
Prepared by Marie Livingston Roy

Chapter 1—Forgiving
For Group Discussion
1. The author suggests that "all honorings of the good . . . may add to the general power of good" and similarly, "wrong choices, indulged glooms, relished hates all have a way of belonging, and together form a network of spreading malevolence. . . ." Based upon personal experiences, do you agree or disagree with this proposition? Why or why not?
2. What do you perceive to be the differences between uncalculating love and unconditional love? Give examples from your own experiences of each. Do you agree with the author that God's love is not unconditional? Why or why not?
3. The author suggests that to "forgive and forget" is unrealistic. Why do you agree or disagree with this concept?
4. How have you come to grips with the unforgiven and unforgivable in the world?

For Personal Reflection
1. According to the author, the miracle of forgiveness occurs when we are able to bear an injury without having our love diminished; when there is only richer love where evil has been. Have you experienced giving or receiving that miracle of forgiveness? What effect, if any, did it have upon your life? the lives of those around you?

2. What do you consider necessary for peace and joy in your life? Of these elements, which could you lose and still experience peace and joy?

3. In what ways have you been able to accept the circumstances of the world as being in God's hands and therefore worthy of trust and hope? In what ways is that acceptance difficult for you? What in your life moves you toward that acceptance?

Chapter 2—Hoping
For Group Discussion

1. The author describes that moment of vision when we come to the end of the line and truth is revealed, when our mistakes become clear, but, also, we "at last see the way through." When have you experienced such moments of vision? What did you learn through them?

2. Do you agree or disagree that "people suspect that the conclusions to which life has quietly been leading them are not very hopeful"? Give examples as to why or why not.

3. What is your response to the statement, "Joy is something you can, if you wish, just let happen to you, but suffering is a load of work that must be done"?

4. If the ability to hope is indeed not the result of effort but of contemplation, what are the implications for today's fast-paced society?

5. What signs of hope do you see within your family? your neighborhood? your faith community? your city? your state? your country?

For Personal Reflection

1. What experiences do you call to mind of persons whose suffering was transformed by hope? What attitudes and actions characterized the experience? How can those attitudes and actions be incorporated into your own life?

2. If you change your orientation from one of *having* to one of *being,* what changes will have to be made in your life? Which ones will be the easiest? the hardest? What sources of encouragement do you think will help the transition most? Why?

3. "Repentance is no denial of one's past; on the contrary, it is a moment of initiation by which the past acquires new meaning." In what ways does your past have new meaning in light of your personal faith journey or "repentance"?

Chapter 3—Belonging
For Group Discussion

1. One of the messages of the image of Mary and John with the crucified Savior is, the author believes, that Christ has "abolished our isolation, particularly the loneliness of pain. We never pray alone." What are the implications of this for the church in today's lonely, pain-filled world? What are some immediate implications for your own faith community?

2. Antonia White said, "If the church is what she claims to be, she *should* be full of the most mixed, uncongruous and mutually antipathetic human beings." In what ways does the church embody this image? Where does it fall short? In what ways does your own faith community embody it? fall short?

3. What are your personal expectations for your community of faith? Do you expect life within the church to be free from the hostilities and disappointments inherent in secular life? Why or why not? In what ways are your expectations met? In what ways are they disappointed? What expectations may need to be re-evaluated?

4. Discuss the following quote: "It is, moreover, a world in which success carries such prestige that any form of suffering, even misfortune like physical illness or bereavement, is easily construed as one of the thousand species of failure. One is vaguely guilty at feeling low when the world throbs away with the vibration of so many cheerful people doing each (their) own robust thing." Using personal experiences as a reference, do you agree or disagree? What role does the church play in supporting or denying this attitude?

For Personal Reflection

1. Jesus' giving of his mother and his disciple to each other is seen by many Christians as a symbol of the mother church and the disciple-family of Jesus. What influence has this symbolism had on the life of the church? Has it influenced your spiritual life? In what way?

2. When have you experienced the loving concern of the unseen family of the community of faith (past, present, and future) in the midst of your suffering? What was the result of that awareness?

3. The author states that "for most of us it is necessary . . . that what we think of God . . . should be focused in an image, to which we return again and again, a kind of landmark in the mind. . . ." What images help you think of God?

4. In Mary's standing at the foot of the cross during Jesus' suffering, the author sees an expression of the grace to remain with pain, even in a hopeless situation, and living it through. In your own experience, have you found it to be true or false that "staying with the grim situation is made easier by thinking no further than the next few moments"? How do you respond to this idea?

5. "Be it done unto me according to thy word"—Mary's words at the annunciation—express openness to God as one who is utterly trustworthy and loving. In what areas of your life are you ready to say these words? In what areas do you resist that affirmation of God as trustworthy and caring? What do you see as encouraging you to surrender those areas?

Chapter 4—Protesting
For Group Discussion

1. The author comments that "It is a pity that the prayer of protest, so clear in the Bible and consecrated by the Saviour's use of it, is so infrequent in the public prayer of the Church." What value do you see in the use of the prayer of protest within the church as a whole? within your own faith community? Identify several situations which seem to call for prayer of protest at this time.

2. Do you agree or disagree with the author that genuine Christian emotion needs to be expressed in public Christian prayer? Why or why not?

3. In what ways do you feel conflict can be a form of deep mutual involvement and unity within your faith community? within your own faith journey?

4. Reflect upon the following quote, then respond to it from your personal experience: "The work of suffering involves drawing on one's inner resources to find the ability to let go what life has taken, to accept the change made by its absence, and to achieve a new position from which life continues to be possible. The result of this work is the growth of the spirit, which we believe is a large amount of what living is for."

For Personal Reflection

1. At what point in your life is the Holy calling you to respond at this time? Are you responding eagerly or with protest? Why?

2. Have you ever expressed a deep, personal cry of protest against an unacceptable situation? What was the result? In retrospect, where do you perceive God's presence in the situation?

3. In what situations have you suffered, struggled to make sense of it, and continued to believe? In retrospect, do you feel that your faith is stronger now than then? Why or why not?

What helped you persevere in your situation? What do you feel you can call on in the future to strengthen you in your distress?

Chapter 5—Wanting
For Group Discussion

1. The author states, "The correction of materialism, as that of 'selfishness,' is not a matter of direct attack. It is a discovery and exploration of that for which a consumer society is really hungry and thirsty while ignorantly and in unconscious despair it tries to make do with things and money." If this is true, what are the implications of this statement for individual Christians? the church? your particular faith community? What does this have to suggest about the solution to rampant consumerism and world hunger?

2. According to the author, "Self-interest, self-concern, in the sense of attempting to know oneself and meet its needs, is part of the work of the spiritual life." He suggests that this self-interest is distinctly different from selfishness. What do you perceive to be the difference between the two? How does self-interest contribute to spiritual growth? How does selfishness impede it?

3. What do you think the author means by suggesting that "Most of the wrongness of life is due to our not wanting love enough, due to our losing heart and settling for less, for what is, however fashionable, a wretched stand-in for love"? How might we learn to want love more? What role does the church play in stirring up the desire for that love? in providing it? What is the responsibility of the Christian in seeking it? giving it?

4. In what ways have you been taken by surprise at the goodness of life? Do you think that our understanding of the goodness of life is in any way dependent upon our willingness to accept its presence when it is made known to us? Why or why not?

For Personal Reflection

1. The author states that "We shall never understand ourselves without becoming quite familiar with our world of wanting." What is it that you want more than anything else from

life? What draws you, motivates you, inspires you? Are there ways you can think of in which your material wants can reflect and even contribute to your spiritual ones?

2. Try to get in touch with what experiences deeply satisfy you and which do not. What means are available to you to increase the satisfying aspects of your life and diminish the sources of dissatisfaction?

3. If, indeed, we can live with dignity only if we live on a few things, chosen for the way they speak deeply to us, what is it that speaks most deeply to you at this point in your spiritual journey? What steps can you take to ensure the continuing of that choice in the face of day-to-day living?

Chapter 6—Achieving
For Group Discussion
1. What difference does the fact that we are to truly carry on the work begun by Jesus (the offering of ourselves to God and being open to all of life) make in your daily living?
2. What do you think the author means by saying that staying with life's situations, trying to dignify them with a bit of meaning, is certain to put movement in them? Do your personal experiences agree or disagree with his statement? Why or why not?
3. The author suggests that we cannot watch our progress in responsiveness to life inside and outside ourselves, or measure it, or make it happen. "It is done," he says, "by God, by love, and always when we ourselves are not looking." By what means, then, can we know when we are achieving spiritual growth?
4. A life lived fully for God and in openness to all of life is exciting, winsome, and easily recognized by others. In whom do you find deep roots of genuine love and joy and peace? What effect does that person, living or dead, have upon your own faith journey? What is it that you want to emulate?

For Personal Reflection
1. What meaning does the Eucharist have for you in your spiritual journey at this time?
2. Jesus was continually able to find hopefulness in the midst of failure. From your own experience, what signs of hope have you discovered in the midst of failure?
3. Reflect upon the passage below; then identify yourself in the relationship or relationships which most characterize your faith journey at this time.

> The friends of Jesus must have found living with him a similar perplexity. For them he was a way of seeing their world for the first time. The fact that a man like him existed at all made life a new thing altogether; that they knew he wanted them made it infinitely important. And his way of living in the present,

without the drag of yesterday, without the dread of what might be coming, yet with beliefs, habits, hopes that suggested a man whose most trivial action was a response to an inner ordering of his whole life—all this produced a peculiar silence in them and the sense that they were being led towards events and experiences for which they had no attitudes prepared. Yet go with him, in love, they must. It was their desire. They frequently quarreled among themselves and with him, often wondered how much longer they could put up with the endless work of understanding him and what he so desperately seemed to want them to understand. They would think of shaking free; and then would come the heavy tug of a deeper truth, that they absolutely belonged to him, a truth made joyful by his extraordinary power of convincing them that what they were was absolutely worth going on with and that what they could yet be was all in the summons and promise of the love that moves the sun and the other stars.

Chapter 7—Giving
For Group Discussion

1. The faith in God that saw Jesus through was not a guarantee that he would not fall, but the certainty that when he fell he would not be alone. This is the same relationship offered to us by God. Are you agreeable to these terms? How would you change them and why? What do you think would be the result if suddenly all the suffering in the world ceased?

2. How do you respond to the author's statement that faith that passes away because of something unpleasant happening to you could not be true faith as Christians understand faith? Do you find it truthful? harsh? Would you qualify it?

3. Discuss the author's statement that failure to love is a death more significant than bodily death.

4. "To this perennial human perplexity Jesus brought faith in the unchanging . . . presence of God, in the rightness of trusting life to be working for you all the time, in the unnecessariness of fear. As this faith is steadily worked into daily experience, our hidden dreads and angers begin to dissolve and our power to love and give is released." What experiences have you had that agree with this statement? Were they difficult? What effect can you see in your life because of them? Do you find that new difficulties are handled with more faith than before? What observations can you make about them that might be helpful to someone else in a similar situation?

5. What aspects of Christian suffering have you encountered in this book that you wish to incorporate into the life of your faith community? into your own life?

For Personal Reflection

1. Our ability to love and give is blocked most by our fears and antipathies. What do you think may be blocking your ability to love and give to the fullest? What ways do you see in which you can overcome these things?

2. "The Christian life is not a preparation for anything; it is a learning how to live here and now in freedom from fear and self-concern, in open faith and hope and love." If you repeated this statement each day as an affirmation of faith, what changes do you think you would make in your day-to-day living as a result?

3. To say "Father, into thy hands I commit my spirit" is to accept the risk of life. Every experience is an opportunity of giving oneself to (God) by doing, enjoying, enduring whatever work or delight or pain the situation carries. At what points in your life can you say "Father, into thy hands I commit my spirit"? At what points are you reluctant? What does this suggest to you as next steps in your spiritual journey?